And My Name Is John

THE BLESSINGS OF SOBRIETY

JOHN DELONG

PAGE PUBLISHING
Conneaut Lake, PA

First originally published by Page Publishing 2024

ISBN 979-8-89315-148-0 (pbk)
ISBN 979-8-89315-173-2 (digital)

Printed in the United States of America

A RAINY NIGHT AFTER A DAY AT WIMBLEDON

Probably the most incredible meeting I have ever been to took place on a trip to Wimbledon a few years back.

I was there for the tennis first and foremost and didn't really plan on making any meetings in London, but for some reason, I was out of sorts all day that particular day. Maybe I was still suffering the aftereffects of the flight over and was going through hungry, angry, lonely, and tired. Who knows?

Anyway, after I got back to the hotel from Wimbledon that evening, I knew that I had to find an eight o'clock meeting to snap out of the funk. I went online to see if any meetings were in the area, and I was totally confused by all the SW7 and NW12 locations; fortunately, the hotel concierge helped me out, and it turned out there was a meeting six or seven blocks away. Thing was, meetings in London start at 7:00 p.m., not 8:00, and it was about 6:55 at the time. It had started to rain, so I went out and walked the six or seven blocks to the Abbey Road Community Center, getting there drenched.

I got there probably five minutes after 7:00, and there was one lady in the lobby. I asked her if there was a meeting, and she said it looked like we were the only ones who weren't scared off by the rain and that we could have a two-person meeting if I wanted. I said yes, so we got out the literature and read the steps and traditions, etc. A few minutes later, a young guy walked in and said he was looking for a meeting, so we wound up with three.

The format for the night was supposed to be a *The Big Book* study, where we would take turns reading from *The Big Book* and then have a discussion at the end. The lady read a few paragraphs. Then I read a few paragraphs. Then the young guy passed. The lady read a few more paragraphs. I read a few more paragraphs. Then the young guy passed again. This continued, and I must admit, the lady and I were both looking at this guy like, "What's the deal? There's just three of us here. Do your part. Why did you even come if you're not going to participate?"

So the reading finally ended, and the lady started the discussion. She said she wanted to thank us so much for coming because she needed a meeting so badly, and she was afraid that she was going to be the only one to show up. She talked out her troubles and had a really good share. Then I started and told about how I was in a funk and needed a meeting so bad and thanked them for being there and shared a little more. So finally, it was the young guy's turn, and to be honest, we didn't know if he was going to share at all or just pass again.

Then came the stunner. "I'm sorry I had to pass every time, but I don't know how to read," he said. "But thank you so much for being here for me because I really, really needed a meeting so bad." Then he talked about moving to London from Dublin recently and how he was still looking to fit into meetings in London and still didn't know anybody and how much sobriety meant to him.

Obviously, the lady and I felt this tall for assuming that he didn't want to participate. What transpired from there was a case of the three of us bonding and sharing our experience, strength, and hope with each other and truly coming out of the funks we had been in. We all left happy, joyous, and free again, inspired by the meeting. The rest of my trip was fabulous.

What I look back at now, and what I think we all realized at the time, is this—if the lady hadn't waited around past seven o'clock, none of this would have happened. If I hadn't shown up, the lady would have been long gone before the young guy got there, and none of this would have happened. If the young guy hadn't shown up, the lady and I would have never learned the valuable lesson that you should never assume something if a person doesn't, or can't, participate in a meeting. Instead of looking down on the young guy for not reading, we suddenly were moved by his courage to go to any lengths to get to a meeting. If any one of us hadn't shown up, none of us would have gotten the relief we so desperately needed.

There was no question that God put us in each other's lives for that evening, for that one moment, to where we could all be inspired and comforted. We all left knowing, too, that there are no coincidences. God and the program truly were working in our lives that rainy evening. A black woman from London, a young guy from Dublin, and a fat, bald American sportswriter—three who, as *The Big Book* says, would not normally mix—had come together to celebrate and grow their sobriety.

A FAMILY OF ESKIMOS SHOWS UP IN ROME

I usually consider myself a pretty savvy traveler.

I know my way around New York, Los Angeles, Chicago, and San Francisco. I fully understand the subway systems in London and Paris. I've even figured out all those canal-lined back alleys in Venice.

But my first trip to Rome earlier this summer had me more than a bit apprehensive. Doing my homework before the trip, I felt daunted by the transportation system there, especially since I was staying at a Marriott property far from the heart of the city, and even more so because I didn't know how to speak even the basics of Italian and wasn't sure how many folks in Rome spoke English.

There's a train system and a Metro subway system in Rome, and from the hotel, it was going to be necessary to master both just to get to landmarks like the Colosseum, Roman Forum, and Vatican City.

The lady at the hotel front desk mapped it all out for me, but excuse me if I still felt completely uncomfortable and overwhelmed. To get to the train station, I was supposed to take a right out of the hotel, then another right at the first street, then another right at the next light. Then I was supposed to take the train all the way to the last stop, and then board a different train until it got to a certain Metro stop, and then switch over to the Metro and take it to the Colosseum stop.

Then, hopefully, I could get on a Hop-On, Hop-Off tour bus and ride around the city and get my bearings down at that point.

Well, there was this initial problem. I took a right out of the hotel, then another right at the first street, then another right at the next light. And I looked and looked for a train station. It was supposed to be right there, but all I saw were cars zipping past me and a lot of barren wasteland. I looked and looked for what I thought should be a fairly obvious train station and couldn't find it at all.

I stood at the street corner, starting to panic, trying to comprehend how this confusing journey had gotten off to such a bad start that I couldn't even find the train station. I didn't know if I should keep on walking or go back to the hotel or what.

And then, out of nowhere, a family of three appeared at the street corner.

I could tell that they were Americans and that gave me some relief, so I asked, "Can you tell me where the train station is?"

The lady said, "Sure, it's right down here," pointing to a valley about fifty yards down that I had assumed was just a wasteland.

"Follow us," she said.

It got even better.

She asked where I was planning to go, and I told her the Colosseum, and it turned out that's where they were going too. They had been to Rome before, were also staying at the hotel, understood the train and subway system, and were more than happy to let me tag along and follow them. We made it to the Colosseum, and by then I was feeling much more comfortable about the entire transportation system and how I would eventually make it back to the hotel.

I thanked them over and over and over as godsends. And that's exactly what they were. A family from the Pittsburgh area, showing up on a street corner in Rome, suddenly appearing and changing my entire day. After they showed me the ropes, I was comfortable enough to head out on my own, and I wound up having a fabulous day.

In recovery, there's a term for people who suddenly show up out of nowhere, make an important impact of one sort or another, and then disappear into the sunset. They're called Eskimos. Truly, it is as if they are sent by God for a specific purpose, and then they are gone. I was called an Eskimo once by someone in Paris who wanted to take a fifth step with somebody he had never seen before and would never see again. I wound up being that guy.

In the program, we believe that God works through people, and I believe wholeheartedly that God puts various people in our lives at different points, even if ever so briefly, to accomplish His will. And what is so neat is to see such a situation play out and know that God is working in our lives. To people that say it was merely a coincidence, I ask, why is it that there are so many coincidences in my life all the time?

There are many things about the Bible that confuse me or seem like contradictions, and there are many things about Jesus that I definitely don't understand. I have a hard time figuring out what in the Bible is to be taken literally and what is to be taken figuratively. I'm still not buying Noah's Ark or the Book of Revelation.

But I absolutely, without any question, believe in guardian angels and Eskimos. It is just impossible to deny their existence.

Without a guardian angel, I would be dead or locked up in a jail somewhere, or at the very least, I would be living a life of fear, remorse, and disillusionment. I've been in automobile accidents. I've driven in blackouts. I've chugged a bottle of tequila in four chugs over fifteen minutes, which should have killed me from alcohol poisoning. I should have been fired from not one but several jobs. I've lived a pathetic, wretched lifestyle at times. All this only to be given second chance after second chance after second chance.

Without an Eskimo, I would still be standing on a street corner in Rome looking for the train station.

I am so grateful.

A LESSON COURTESY OF IL DIVO AND SUPERTRAMP

I have a rather large collection of concert DVDs ranging from Eric Clapton to Steely Dan to the Eagles to Seal to James Taylor to Stevie Wonder to Elton John to Roger Waters to Peter Frampton and on and on and on.

The collection is so large, in fact, that for years there was only one group missing that I really, really wanted: Supertramp, one of my favorite bands from the '80s.

It seemed that there was only one Supertramp concert DVD in existence, and it was poor quality from a concert early in their careers, prior to many of the band's greatest hits. I looked and looked for it at every music store in town, and once I even tried to special order it, to no avail. It was out of stock, and nobody was going to make any more copies.

Supertramp broke up in bitterness, and there is no way the group would ever get back together for a reunion tour or anything, so I accepted the reality that my DVD collection would always be a little incomplete. No "Breakfast in America." No "Take the Long Way Home." No "Dreamer."

And then came Christmas a few years ago.

I was at the mall and had done all my Christmas shopping and was about to head home when I decided I probably needed one more little stocking stuffer for my mom. Called my sister, and she suggested a new CD by Il Divo, a group I had never heard of but was apparently one of my mom's favorites.

So I went to the music store, found the particular Il Divo CD, and was about to go to the checkout counter. But suddenly, something else caught my eye.

The CDs and DVDs were all in alphabetical order. And right there next to *I* was *H*. And for some reason, the H DVDs started with a Roger Hodgson DVD. That's Roger Hodgson, as in the lead singer and chief songwriter for Supertramp.

He has been touring on his own the past few years and had put out his own concert DVD live from Montreal that was great quality and had all my favorite songs!

I was thrilled, naturally, and bought it on the spot. Then I went home and played it, and it was great, and I have been enjoying it ever since.

But what thrilled me even more was the lesson I took out of the experience.

I had searched and searched for a Supertramp concert DVD for years and had always come up empty. It had never dawned on me to look for a Roger Hodgson DVD. Yet when the day came that I wasn't searching for it, and was instead thinking of someone else, God delivered something that was even better than what I had been hoping for. I would have settled for an old, muffled concert DVD from the '80s with poor sound quality, and instead I got pure sound, all the hits, done by someone who was clearly enjoying being back out on tour.

Tells me exactly what the program says. When you get out of yourself and try to do something nice for somebody else instead, unexpected blessings flow your way. And sometimes, what you think you want is not nearly as neat as what God has in mind for you.

We alcoholics forget that all too often. So it's nice to have tangible reminders.

Sure, it's only a DVD, one of more than a hundred in my collection nowadays. But what it represents is far greater than that. It gives me pause, and it gives me hope that if I just go about my business the right way, God will indeed have plenty in store for me. For that, I am so grateful.

AN EMAIL THAT CHANGED MY LIFE

I had put my work ahead of my sobriety for years and years. It was understandable in some ways because it was such a great job, a job that God had no doubt blessed me with. It's hard to go to a lot of meetings when you're in Boston one night, New York the next, back home for three days, then off to Miami and Orlando after that and on and on for seven months out of the year.

But the bottom line is, my sobriety suffered in those years, and I wasn't living the program to the fullest. Did plenty of stupid and regrettable things, wasn't "practicing these principles in all my affairs" like the twelfth step demands. I was a guy who knew how not to drink, but I was basically staying sober on the first step alone in many cases.

I knew I had to somehow, some way, get back into the program full-bore and make sobriety my top priority again.

Then came an email. It was from a friend I had gone to high school with, someone I hadn't seen or talked to in more than thirty years. She had moved to town and had seen my column picture and email address in the newspaper. She was writing to reconnect, suggested we get together for coffee some time.

I was petrified. We had partied like rock stars in the old days, and frankly, I was still ashamed of so much of the stupid stuff I had done back then. How much of that did she remember? I was sure she remembered me as this wild-and-crazy drunk that made a fool of himself often. I appeased her by saying yes, we'd do coffee sometime, but in my heart, there was no way I was ever going to follow through with it.

Weeks later, her father died. I knew her father from when I had played baseball with her brothers growing up. I sent an email with my condolences, offering up a little support since my dad had died unexpectedly years before. She thanked me and remarked that we were now members of the Dead Dad's Club together.

God stepped in at that point. For some reason, I was compelled to tell her that I was in another club, a club where we share our experience, strength, and hope. I told her my experience was that she would have some really rough days, but it would get easier as time went on, and that in the process she would get closer to her family and would appreciate each day a little more, and that my hope was that she would deal with her grief and some kind of good would come out of it.

Imagine my surprise when she replied with a big exclamation point that she knew what club I was talking about, and she was in that club too. We were fellow trudgers. She had been in the program for several years.

Well, at that point, getting together for coffee became a must. And it turned into a regular occurrence. And I started going to her home group, where the meetings were fabulous. And it spurred me to make that total recommitment to the program, and I was able to really, truly jump back into the program full-bore at that point.

For the past six years, recovery and meetings and working with others have been my primary focus again. I'm working the program the way it's supposed to be worked. Our friendship has grown and thrived, and there's that deep appreciation and bond that all recovering alcoholics can relate to. We lean on each other for support when we need it. We talk of spiritual growth. We share the happy, joyous, and free that the program promises.

Her DDC day—the anniversary of her dad's death—was earlier this week. It was a sad day but also a joyous one as she celebrated his life and all the good memories and all the love she has for him.

My reward has been her friendship, and the knowledge that her loss was the catalyst for me to really get full-bore back into the program and put sobriety back at the top of my priorities. In recovery, we call that God doing for us what we could not do for ourselves. I am so grateful.

WHEN THE STUDENT IS READY, THE TEACHER WILL APPEAR

Sneaky folks, the French.

When you walk into one of the English-speaking meetings in Paris, there's a good chance that somebody will approach you and ask you to tell your story. All meetings there begin with a twenty-minute share, or "lead" as they call it, and when an American tourist walks in, the chairperson inevitably jumps at the opportunity to hear a new speaker.

That is precisely what happened to me at my very first meeting in Paris. I went thinking that I could just chill and observe; suddenly, I was front and center talking about what it used to be like, what happened, and what it's like now.

I have to say, it was one of the most emotional experiences of my life.

I don't remember everything that I shared, but I do remember sitting there awed and inspired. Here I was, a guy who used to drink a fifth a day during the worst of times, who lived in a tiny apartment that was a dump, who had no money and bounced checks on Wednesday to buy liquor until payday on Friday, who had all his credit cards cut off, who was lucky he hadn't been fired from his job long before, whose friends cared about him but were ashamed for him, a guy who basically felt hopeless and full of shame and misery—yes, here I was telling how God and sobriety had changed my life. At a meeting *in Paris*!

I felt a sense of gratitude and happy, joyous, and free that cannot be adequately described. Definitely one of the neatest moments of my life. A feeling that I wish everyone in recovery could experience at least once.

That's not the best part.

At the meeting that day was an American expat who had only been sober a few months. He didn't have a sponsor. He had never shared a single time at a meeting. He had not made any friends in the program. He was basically showing up for the meetings and nothing else, and for that reason, he was stuck on the fourth step and not sure how to proceed.

His ears perked up when I told my sobriety date and where I was from. He had lived in the same city years before. It was the first crack in the door for him. After the meeting, he introduced himself, and for the first time, opened up and talked about his struggles in early sobriety. We had a great conversation and basically laid out a game plan for him to get a sponsor and really throw himself into the program.

Long story short, we have become great friends in the years since, and now he is not only an active member of the fellowship, but he is one of the real stalwarts of the Paris 12-step recovery community. This shy guy who sat in the back is now carrying the message, living the program to the fullest. In the time since, it has become a tradition for him to host seventy-five to eighty recovering expats for a sober Fourth of July party each summer at his home in the shadows of the Eiffel Tower. I couldn't be prouder of him or happier for him.

We know there are no coincidences. We know that, as the program teaches us, when the student is ready, the teacher will appear. That's how I feel God used me that day, to help crack the door open simply by stating where I lived and then talking to a newcomer afterward. For my friend, it was a case of God doing for him what he could not do for himself—and a case of him taking action for the first time in his sobriety by introducing himself and sharing about his struggles.

Amazing program, isn't it?

And a pretty good reason to keep going back to Paris. You never know what might happen at a meeting.

STAYING SOBER ONE VENTI VANILLA
BEAN FRAPPUCCINO AT A TIME

I am sitting in a Starbucks near my home on a sunny Easter Sunday afternoon, enjoying a Venti Vanilla Bean Frappuccino. I have just come to a wonderful realization.

Starbucks, to me, is not just an overpriced coffee shop. It's a priceless aid to my sobriety, a setting and an atmosphere where I can sit back and relax, reflect, refocus, reaffirm, or recharge my emotional and spiritual batteries as the situation warrants.

We talk in recovery about using the various tools in the toolbox to stay sober, whether it be praying or reading *The Big Book* or going to meetings or calling your sponsor or helping others or summoning up hundreds of other little tricks we have learned over the years.

Strange as it might sound, a visit to Starbucks is definitely one of those countless tools.

It goes well beyond the fact that coffee is the official drink of 12-step programs everywhere.

At Starbucks, the background music is generally very soothing. Not exactly elevator music but usually a hip, 2015 version. There is peace and calm, a tranquility in the air. There is a vitality to it, no doubt, with customers coming and going, but at the same time, the setting invites you to stop and—pun intended—smell the coffee.

The people are always happy and cheerful. There is a spirit of good will everywhere. Have you ever heard an argument in a Starbucks, or even a raised voice for that matter? I find that chilling out and doing a little people-watching, especially when people are in such good moods, can be uplifting in itself.

For some reason, a half hour at Starbucks seems to draw the gratitude out in me. I have sat in a Starbucks in Sausalito overlooking the Golden Gate Bridge and San Francisco Bay, and I have thought to myself, "There's no place in the world I would rather be than right here, right now." The same thought has hit me at the Starbucks on the Royal Mile in Edinburgh, and the one across the street from the Louvre in Paris, and the one just a short walk beyond Abbey Road in London, and the original Starbucks in Seattle of course. And so many more.

So whenever I'm in a Starbucks, I automatically think of all the wonderful things I've been able to do in my life because of sobriety.

What strikes me as I sit here writing this is that the tools in the sobriety toolbox do indeed come in many shapes and forms. Thousands, literally many, and totally unique to each person. And they develop over time.

If I told a newcomer that spending part of my day at Starbucks is one of the things that helps keep me sober, it would sound absurd. Yet it is true. It works. It's a great place where I can go when I'm down in the dumps, when I need to hit the reset button, and get back on the right track; and it's also a great place where I can go when I am happy, joyous, and free and want to enjoy the moment.

I'll take a Venti Vanilla Bean Frappuccino over a fifth of misery anytime.

FEDERER, THE EIFFEL TOWER, AND CARRYING THE MESSAGE

This has been another fun and productive trip to Europe.

I have watched lots of great tennis at the French Open. I have had lunch in the Latin Quarter. I have prayed inside Sacre Coeur, walked along the Seine and down the Champs Elysees, hung out at the Eiffel Tower, and hit so many other fabulous landmarks in Paris.

I have navigated Rome for the first time, which includes being awestruck at the Colosseum, walking through the Roman Forum, visiting the Vatican, and again hitting all the other major landmarks. I have feasted on pasta and probably gone a little overboard on the pistachio gelato.

The most important thing I did on this trip, however, had nothing to do with Notre Dame or the Trevi Fountain or even Roger Federer.

The most important thing I did on this trip was help give someone hope.

It happened at the noon meeting at the American Cathedral in Paris, which has become my home-away-from-home group of sorts.

It was supposed to be a meeting on the fourth step, but midway through, a lady probably in her midthirties raised her hand to share (that's the way they do it in Paris.) She said it was her fourth day sober. She talked passionately about how badly she wanted to quit drinking, how desperately she wanted to believe that the program would work, how she was trying to hang on one day at a time, and how she would appreciate all the phone numbers and support she could get.

Cue me. It was time to share some experience, strength, and hope.

When my chance to share came, I pointed to the tradition—each group has one primary purpose, to carry the message to the alcoholic who still suffers. And without crossing the line that would be considered crosstalk, I aimed the message directly at her.

The newcomer, I said, was in fact the most important person in the group. And the message for the newcomer is that if your drinking is totally out of control and you are sick and tired of being sick and tired, and if you want to quit more than anything in the world, and if you are willing to go to any lengths to get sober, well, let there be no doubt that the program really, truly, absolutely works.

It absolutely works—if you work it.

I told her every one of the thirty or so people in the room could vouch for the fact that the program worked, that none of us would be sitting in a meeting in Paris saying it did if it wasn't true. I told her there were more than two million recovering alcoholics from all parts of the world who had seen their lives change dramatically because of the program.

I told her of my early days in recovery, when I wound up in treatment at my lowest point ever, fearing that I was ruined professionally and unable to look my friends in the eye because of shame. I didn't know anything about the twelve steps. I didn't know anything about sponsors or meetings or service work or anything else. I just knew that I absolutely, positively had to stop drinking.

I told her how I had been intimidated by the steps when I first read them. I clearly had taken the first step—admitted we were powerless over alcohol and that our lives had become unmanageable—but I was scared of the third step, wasn't sure I was ready to turn my will and life over to the care of God. My heart actually sank a little when I initially saw that word *God*, because I had conveniently kept him at arm's length throughout my drinking career.

But, I said, I know now that the steps are in order for a reason, that it's okay if you can't take the third step right off the bat. I know now that when it's time to deal with God, God will give you the pathway. That all it takes to get started is the first step and some honesty, willingness, and open-mindedness.

And finally, I told her, as others before me had also shared, how the program had completely turned my life around and how I had been showered with blessings beyond my wildest dreams in the years since I had gotten sober. Here I was, a guy who lived in a rathole apartment in my drinking days, bouncing checks on Wednesday to get enough liquor to last till payday on Friday, morally and spiritually bankrupt, full of guilt and shame and hopelessness, and today I lived in my dream house, had financial security, owned an enviable art collection, had a good job, had the respect of friends and family, and was visiting Europe for the umpteenth time.

All this in less than four minutes, which is the limit for sharing in Paris meetings.

After the meeting, she approached me and thanked me for my share. And then, she added that she was so moved by it that she almost cried, that it had given her the hope that she was desperately needing. I wished her well and reassured her one more time that the program really did work, and she had so much to look forward to.

I'll tell you this. There is no better feeling in the world than encouraging a newcomer and feeling that you might have made a difference. This is what we do. We pass on what was so freely given us, and we find that in giving it away we are filled with joy and gratitude and a sense of purpose.

I will never forget what it was like to get a glimmer of hope in my early days of recovery. It was the most important thing that could have happened to me. I had truly felt I was hopeless when I got to rehab, and the notion that I could climb out of the hole I had dug for myself was no doubt a divine spark. The lectures all made sense. Reading *The Big Book* was so powerful, because it described me—my insides and my outsides—better than I could describe myself. How did they know that much about me, all my emotions and reactions and the various troubles I had gotten into? I figured if they could describe me so perfectly, maybe they knew what they were talking about when they outlined a path to sobriety and all the promises they guaranteed.

That's how I got my hope back, and sure enough, all those promises eventually came true.

So what had started out as a fourth step meeting in Paris actually turned into a second step meeting. The second step is the step of hope. It's not merely coming to believe in a higher power, it's coming to believe that a higher power can restore us to sanity. Sanity as in not drinking and trying to do the next right thing and eventually establishing and maintaining a relationship with God and living a full and prosperous life.

This European trip ends tomorrow. I saw Federer. I sat on Colosseum granite that had been in the same place for two thousand years. I carried the message. Fun and productive, for sure.

THE STORY OF THE ALCOHOLIC SKY-DIVING CAT

In my drinking days (years), I had the nickname "Gonzo," in reference to the writer Hunter S. Thompson and his infamous Gonzo journalism. The concept was to get as drunk or high as possible and then write whatever stream of consciousness that popped into your head. He was really good at it. I was really good at the first part.

So after I got sober, a friend talked me into getting a kitten. It was only natural to name him "Gonzo Junior."

Junior was a great cat—cute as could be with a great personality. I'd never had a cat before, and I must say that he was all the good things we know about cats and none of the bad.

There was one thing though.

Over time, I came to realize that Junior was every bit the alcoholic that I was. He didn't drink a fifth of bourbon a day, of course, but he had all the isms of addiction. He loved having fun, he loved getting a rush, and once he got that feeling, he would do it over and over and over.

I had a multilevel condo with a sunken living room at the time. There was a loft above. So the actual distance from the upstairs to the sunken living room was probably thirty feet at least, probably more.

Junior would go up to the top of the loft, then would jump off and go flying through the air, like Rocky the Flying Squirrel from the Bullwinkle cartoons. He would land on my leather couch, which softened the landing, and after each leap, he would strut around like he had just done the neatest thing in the world.

Eventually, the inevitable happened. There would be times when he landed on the couch, but there were other times when he would miss the couch and crash land on either the coffee table or the carpet.

He'd stagger around, dazed and confused and clearly hurting, and I would tell him, "Junior, you've got to quit doing that, you're going to kill yourself."

It wouldn't be long before he had shaken it off and was back to the top of the loft, ready to fly through the air again.

Isn't that the truest description of an alcoholic? Doing the same thing over and over and hoping for different results. Chasing the rush regardless of the costs, regardless of all the pain and suffering that comes afterward. Being unable to stop even when you want to and need to.

Sadly enough, the times when he landed on the couch became fewer and fewer, and the times when he crash landed into the coffee table became more and more. It finally got to the point where he'd been beaten up enough and knew he couldn't continue any longer.

By the time Junior realized that, though, it was too late. He wound up with internal injuries from the crash landings, and I had to take him to the vet to be put away. One of the saddest days of my life was the day I had to take him to the vet. Initially there was hope that they'd be able to save him, but I remember vividly during the drive to the vet, he looked at me as if he knew it was over.

In *The Big Book*, there's a story about the jaywalker who continues to jaywalk even after getting hit numerous times, breaking multiple bones in the process. Junior was my living example of what that story tried to illustrate—the progressiveness of our disease and the ultimate fatality of it.

I am so grateful that I got sober before I died. I am so grateful that I crashed and burned in a way that caught my attention and explained the insanity of alcoholism without so many of the tragic results that could have happened. There was enough madness as it was. I am grateful that I got the gift of desperation before it was too late. That truly is God's grace.

Only recently has it occurred to me that maybe I could have closed off the loft so that Junior couldn't have gotten to the ledge to jump off. Not sure why I didn't think of that back then.

But we know, too, that even if you lock the door to the bar, an active alcoholic is going to find a way to drink somewhere, somehow. And a flying cat is going to find a way to fly. Until it has used up all nine of its lives.

It's a sad story, a sad memory, but ultimately there is a lesson that I will long remember.

THE LIGHT CAN COME ON WHEN
YOU LEAST EXPECT IT

I was sprucing up the master bedroom a while back and decided to buy a couple of new lamps for the nightstands.

Only problem was, I couldn't find what I was looking for. I went online to the websites of several lamp manufacturers, to no avail. I looked at the catalogs of all the old reliables, from Pottery Barn and Restoration Hardware to World Market, etc. I searched and searched for the perfect lamps, and still, nothing struck me.

I didn't particularly want to "settle" and buy something that wasn't exactly what I wanted, but I still wanted to do something.

Eventually, I gave up the search and decided to stick with the lamps I had, at least for the time being.

Well, wouldn't you know. Not long after, I went to Lowes to buy an extension cord and happened to walk past the lighting display. And there it was, a lamp that was absolutely perfect for the room, something that was way, way better than what I'd initially had in mind.

I had never thought to look at Lowes back when I was looking everywhere else, yet lo and behold, that's where the perfect lamps appeared, while I was running an errand and was not even looking for them. Less expensive than I had budgeted too.

That wasn't the end of the story though.

With the master bedroom looking good, I turned my attention toward the formal living room. It needed something to give it a little more pop, and it struck me that the solution was a floor lamp between one of the end tables and the fireplace.

So I went through the same process again, from Pottery Barn to Restoration Hardware, and yes, for sure, to Amazon. Always remember Amazon. And while I was at it, I took another trip to Lowes, just in case they had the perfect floor lamp as well.

No such luck this time, and so my search for the perfect floor lamp hit another roadblock.

I did what I had done before. I quit looking and figured that it wasn't meant to be.

Imagine my surprise when one day I was on the internet, and suddenly, there was a pop-up ad from Wayfair, a company I had never shopped with. And guess what it had? Not just a bunch of floor lamps, but something better than I had seen anywhere. Stained glass with the perfect colors to complement the rest of the room.

I bought it immediately, and when it arrived, it looked even better than the picture.

I couldn't be happier with both of my purchases.

I have to say, the place is looking pretty good these days.

But what I take out of these experiences is a lot more than mere lighting. It's enlightenment.

What both episodes tell me is that if I am patient and do the legwork and don't "settle" for something less than what I really want, God will eventually put something in front of me that is better than I could have imagined.

If I am patient and have an ideal in my mind, be it a lamp or artwork or a new car or a job or anything else, I will indeed find it eventually.

What pleases me the most is that I continually have these types of experiences that I can turn into life lessons. On one level, all I did was buy some lamps. On a very different level, I got another reminder that God is going to look out for me, and He can give me things way better than my expectations if I'm patient enough, and that it can all happen in the blink of an eye when I least expect it.

Those are all very, very reassuring notions that keep me going in tough times.

No doubt, these are first-grade lessons to normal people. These are notions that should come naturally to most. But it takes us longer to learn than the average person, because we were all busy getting hammered when we should have been growing up, and we've been playing catch-up ever since.

I need these reminders in my life. I need these lessons. And I am very, very grateful for them.

IN A NEW YORK STATE OF MIND

I love New York.

I love Central Park and Yankee Stadium and Times Square and Little Italy and Madison Square Garden and Broadway and the Marriott Marquis and the Macy's Thanksgiving Day parade and the US Open tennis tournament, and I could relax on a park bench in Strawberry Fields forever.

But could I stay sober in New York? Could I work a good program in New York?

I always ask myself that question when I'm there, because everything that happens when I'm in New York seems counterproductive to sobriety.

To me, New York is the self-centered capital of the universe, and I get caught up in it almost immediately. If others jaywalk, I jaywalk with them, even if it means dodging cabs. When I'm on the subway, I'm plotting to beat everyone else and get the open seat when somebody stands up to leave. When I'm driving, I'm ten thousand times more likely to flip a bird to a car that cuts in front of me than I would be at home.

I get reeled into the hustle and bustle of New York, and it's me, me, me, me, me. Even when I'm having a great time, the serenity level is quite different than anywhere else I've ever been. Now, the desire to drink is never there—that's simply not an option or even a thought anymore—but I just don't know how much "Easy Does It" and "Live and Let Live" and other slogans I could live by on a daily basis there. From my professional dealings with New Yorkers, it seems to be such a cutthroat lifestyle they live, whether it be on Wall Street or in the ultracompetitive newspaper industry or wherever.

But obviously, many, many New Yorkers get sober and work fantastic programs. I have several good friends in the program who are transplanted New Yorkers, and I have the utmost respect for all of them.

So I posed the question to one of them—is it easier or tougher to get sober in New York?

Interestingly, her answers had nothing to do with pushing folks out of the way on the subway.

Yes, she said, it is tougher in some ways, the biggest reason being that New Yorkers are largely transient and impersonal, so meetings there often lack the fellowship that we consider so vital to recovery. The temptation to isolate and drift away from the program is probably stronger there than in smaller cities.

But, she said, she couldn't have gotten sober anywhere else. It's easier because there are meetings around the clock, meetings on every other street corner, so there's no excuse for not throwing yourself totally into the program if you want to. The meetings are full of *Big Book* thumpers, not molly-coddlers. Meetings are actually meetings, not counseling sessions. They take their meetings seriously, and obviously that has a profound impact on newcomers.

Of course, we know that an alcoholic can recover anywhere if he or she is willing to go to any lengths. As *The Big Book* says, wife or no wife, job or no job, we can stay sober as long as we are in fit spiritual condition. There are no asterisks that say, "Except in New York."

In fact, in a very different sense I can see how living in New York could speed up the process of hitting bottom, which is the touchstone of recovery. If I would have lived in New York in the '70s and '80s with all the craziness that was going on back then, I surely would have crashed and burned much quicker than I did.

Then again, I might have gotten run over by a cabbie while I was drunk and jaywalking too.

During my drinking years, I had my own form of March Madness.

I would cover NCAA Tournament games, get smashed afterward, cover more NCAA Tournament games, get smashed afterward, cover more NCAA Tournament games, get smashed afterward, and then on the nights when I wasn't covering games, I would get really, really smashed.

That's the life of an alcoholic sportswriter armed with an expense account and access to the media hospitality room. It's a month-long party from one city to the next, "a drunkard's dream if I ever did see one" as the Band puts it.

Never mind the hangovers and the blackouts and all the humiliating moments that sometimes were funny but usually weren't. It was just the cost of doing business.

Today, of course, we in recovery know the futility of that lifestyle. We know that when alcoholics drink alcoholically, it's a progressive disease, and it only gets worse and worse and worse. *The Big Book* suggests that there are three inevitable outcomes: jails, institutions, and death.

The beginning of the end for me came at the Meadowlands in East Rutherford, New Jersey, during the 1987 Eastern Regional. I had partied my way through the ACC Tournament and the NCAA first and second round weekends, and if North Carolina beat Syracuse in the regional final, I would be on to New Orleans for the Final Four.

Usually, with a trip to the Final Four on the line, I would be silently praying for my team to win, rooting for them to advance, because covering the Final Four was the ultimate for a college basketball writer. And so it was as I covered this game. I was on the edge of my seat from the start. I had a vested interest in seeing North Carolina win.

But late in the game, something happened, something that I didn't understand at the time but comprehend and appreciate fully now.

It had been a tight game the whole way, going back and forth with all kinds of emotional swings. In the final minute, North Carolina trailed by two but had possession with an opportunity to tie. They called time out.

I vividly remember sitting there during the time out and suddenly being overwhelmed by a very scary thought. It wasn't the standard, "Please, please, please let Carolina win so I can go to New Orleans." It was, "I don't know if I can survive a week in New Orleans at this point." I honestly didn't know if I had another week of booze and basketball in me, especially in a party city like New Orleans, because I was so beaten down physically and emotionally.

It turned out that Carolina lost, and I can't say that I was happy, but there was a definite feeling of relief that came over me.

Now, that didn't mean that I suddenly saw the light and quit drinking on the spot. But the end was near and a week later, sure enough, I went on the drunk to end all drunks and hit rock bottom. I wound up in the hospital. They wouldn't allow me to check out unless I agreed to go to a treatment center, because they knew this was a classic case of alcoholism gone wild. My recovery started at that point, and the next thirty days in rehab wound up being the most important thirty days of my life.

What I know in retrospect is that during that last time out in the Meadowlands, I let go, or at least started the process of letting go. It took another week of drinking and one more final defining episode for me to fully understand the insanity of alcoholism and say, once and for all, that this craziness had to stop immediately. But it was well worth it.

March Madness has never been the same since. Thank God.

When I moved into my current house about seven years ago, I went through the standard process of meeting all my new neighbors.

Everyone was so welcoming and cordial, as you would expect.

But there was one exception, and her name was Betty.

Betty was the family next door's boxer, and she was having no part of any welcoming party. She growled an angry, mean, vicious growl that made it very clear that she didn't like me or anything about me. The barking started the moment I would come out to the backyard, and it wouldn't stop until I was back inside the house. For days, she was clearly trying to run me off.

So my mission was clear.

Somehow, some way, I was going to have to make peace with this dog, so we could coexist in the same neighborhood.

The answer came in the form of dog biscuits. I would take a handful for her and the family's other dog, a happy-go-lucky Lab named Charlie, and over the course of time, she not only settled down, but she clearly began looking forward to her daily treats.

It got to the point where they would make a mad dash to the fence any time they saw me. Many mornings, they would even start barking to let me know they were outdoors and were ready to get their treats. Over time, it turned out to be a daily ritual—Betty always got fed first, then Charlie, jumping up and down in anticipation, would snatch his biscuit out of the air.

Clearly, I loved the dogs, and they loved me, right up to the day my neighbors moved out of state.

None of this should be an earth-shattering life lesson, especially since it's widely understood that dogs can always be bribed with dog biscuits and, after all, once you win them over, they are the very definition of unconditional love.

But it's one of the best examples in my life of how to deal with others. I wandered into a hostile situation at first, and I diffused the situation by reaching out and being kind. I decided that I was going to make friends with this dog no matter what it took, and in a relatively short period, the conversion took place. Eventually, the love I received in return became a true blessing.

My neighbors later told me that Betty had never been friendly with anyone before I arrived on the scene, that I certainly wasn't the first person to hear that angry, hateful growl. And they said she had never wanted to spend any time outside the house before we struck up our friendship. They loved her, of course, but they said they saw a complete personality change in her once I started showering her with love.

I'm not always that way with people. There's a tendency still to size up a situation and prejudge strangers, and if I believe that they might harm me or are a threat to me, then I still put up all sorts of walls. All too often, if I perceive that someone doesn't like me, then I choose to put up my defenses instead of reaching out and trying to forge a friendship. That's being fear-based instead of doing God's will and loving thy neighbor as thyself.

I know what I should do, though, and I know from experience that it works.

The Big Book says exactly what Betty proved—that if we are kind to others, chances are they will be kind to us. That if we love others, they will eventually love us. That if we look for the good in people, the good will be revealed in due time. That there's a little bit of good in even the worst of us.

And honestly, that's one of the beauties of recovery. We who have made enemies all our lives, and have held grudges, and have had limited social skills, who never particularly took to the Golden Rule, who have barked back at dogs instead of befriending them, now we have a toolbox full of tools to improve all our relationships.

Thank you, God. Thank you, Betty.

I've spent the past few days working on preparations for this summer's trip to Wimbledon, as we currently have twenty-six and counting signed up to go.

It puts me in London mode these days, and that always prompts good memories and neat stories.

One of my favorites came one day, a few years back, when I was walking from landmark to landmark, on a course from the West End to Piccadilly Circus to Trafalgar Square to Buckingham Palace to Westminster Abbey and Big Ben, and on and on.

I'd walked that route many times before, but this time I thought I'd do something different. I was in a really good place spiritually in those days, so I decided that I was going to be on the lookout for all the ways God would reveal Himself to me along the way. Just little God-shots or aha moments as we call them in the program. I didn't know what I was actually looking for, but I figured if I was open to whatever happened, something indeed would happen.

It turned out, there were, in fact, several little God-shots along the way. Sitting in Westminster Abbey and praying and meditating was definitely a spiritual experience.

But the part of the day I think back to the most came while I was strolling through the West End. I walked past a bookstore and something caught my attention—a poster of the *Desiderata*. Now, I'm not sure I had ever read the *Desiderata* before. Back in the '70s, it was the craze, everyone had a *Desiderata* poster, but for some reason, back then I thought it was corny and wanted nothing to do with it.

On this day in London, I stopped to read it. And I was amazed at what I read.

"Go placidly amidst the noise and haste, and remember what peace there may be in silence. As far as possible without surrender be on good terms with all persons. Speak your truth quietly and clearly, and listen to others, even the dull and the ignorant; they too have their story. Avoid loud and aggressive persons, they are vexatious to the spirit. If you compare yourself with others, you may become vain and bitter, for always there will be greater and lesser persons than yourself.

"Enjoy your achievements as well as your plans. Keep interested in your own career, however humble; it is a real possession in the changing fortunes of time. Exercise caution in your business affairs, for the world is full of trickery. But let this not blind you to what virtue there is; many persons strive for high ideals, and everywhere life is full of heroism.

"Be yourself. Especially, do not feign affection. Neither be cynical about love, for in the face of all aridity and disenchantment it is as perennial as the grass. Take kindly the counsel of the years, gracefully surrendering the things of youth. Nurture strength of spirit to shield you in sudden misfortune. But do not distress yourself with dark imaginings. Many fears are born of fatigue and loneliness.

"Beyond a wholesome discipline, be gentle with yourself. You are a child of the universe, no less than the trees and the stars. You have a right to be here. And whether or not it is clear to you, no doubt the universe is unfolding as it should. Therefore be at peace with God, whatever you conceive Him to be, and whatever your labors and aspirations, in the noisy confusion of life keep peace with your soul. With all its shams, drudgery, and broken dreams, it is still a beautiful world. Be cheerful. Strive to be happy."

When I finished reading it, I felt like I had just gone to a meeting. The whole thing is program, program, program, right up to God as you understand Him.

The lesson I got out of that day is this—if I am on the lookout for God's presence, it will be revealed. If I am on the lookout for neat spiritual God-shots, they might come from anywhere, even a bookstore window in London. And there were other little God-shots elsewhere that day as well. It was all a matter of having the awareness to notice and receive them.

Sure, I'm like everyone, I get caught up in the craziness of the day, and I'm not always on the lookout. I'm certain God reveals Himself often, and I am too busy to notice it or fully comprehend it.

But what a neat adventure it can be when I am on the lookout.

THE MORE YOU GIVE, THE MORE YOU RECEIVE

Over the weekend, I volunteered to ring the bell for the Salvation Army out in front of one of the local grocery stores.

I've volunteered for various things in the past but never for the Salvation Army at Christmas, so I was kind of curious about how the day would play out. What percentage of people would contribute? Would people give loose change or dollar bills or bigger denominations? Would it largely be older folks, richer folks, whites, blacks, or what? Would I wind up with a ringing noise in my ears the rest of the night?

I decided I would look for trends as the time progressed, to see if there was a lesson to be learned from the experience.

It didn't take long to get the answer.

The people who contributed had one thing in common—a smile on their face.

They were joyful and friendly and clearly in the Christmas spirit. You could pretty much spot them from the time they got out of their cars and walked toward you. There was an ease about them. Many let their children actually drop the money into the bucket, and the faces on the children lit up as well when they were contributing.

Now, I don't know if they gave because they were in a good mood, or if they were in a good mood because they gave. But I do know the joy was undeniable and infectious.

For the most part, I didn't see that same kind of joy on the faces of those who hurriedly walked past and into the store or, in some cases, quickly looked away as they were walking by in order to avoid eye contact. That's generalizing, but the lesson is still the same.

Charity brings out the best in people. There's a saying in the program that the more you give, the more you receive, and it really is true. Kind of goes hand in hand with the twelfth step, which says you've got to give it away to keep it.

And as anyone who has been in the program can attest, the Salvation Army is particularly worthy with its drug and alcohol abuse programs. I've worked with those in the Salvation Army program, and I've been to their graduation ceremonies and heard the graduates talk about how their lives had changed, and it's so moving.

Just like this weekend was.

EVERYTHING'S COMING UP ROSES

The Rose Bowl was on my bucket list before I even knew what a bucket list was.

When I was growing up, the Rose Bowl was about the biggest deal there was on New Year's Day, especially when my beloved Ohio State Buckeyes played—which was often in those days—and especially when you combined it with the Rose Bowl parade.

Warm and sunny Pasadena seemed like a paradise compared to cold and snowy Ohio. Watching the parade and game on television, there was a Hollywood Tinseltown glamor to it all, a larger-than-life quality to it. To go see it all in person was a dream, but to be honest, it was a dream that I never figured would actually come true.

Guess what? Dreams do come true.

A few years back, the stars aligned, and I was able to fly to Los Angeles for the 2010 Rose Bowl between Ohio State and Oregon. I'd have gone years earlier had it not been for one small problem: Ohio State had not gone to the Rose Bowl in twelve years and had been only twice in the previous twenty-four. Quick reminder: don't take success for granted.

I had some preconceived notions, naturally, particularly about the Tournament of Roses Parade. I thought it would be this magnificent, grandiose parade that was over the top of anything I'd ever experienced. I thought the streets would be lined ten-deep, that the floats would be breathtaking, that the bands would play on and on.

Some of that wound up being true. But much of it was not. The parade had more the feel of the Halloween parade in my small Ohio hometown than it did some time-honored, world-renowned spectacle. While the floats were impressive, they were far more magnificent on television than in real life. There were long stretches between the floats and bands, which I now know as the times where the networks went to commercial breaks. The cameras show the horses, but they don't show the clean-up crews with pooper scoopers that are as much a part of the parade as roses themselves.

I left there thinking I was glad I had seen the parade in person once in my life, but I was not about to put it anywhere near the top of all-time favorites. In fact, I would put the Macy's Thanksgiving Day parade in New York way, way above the Rose Bowl parade. Those balloons coming down Broadway, now that truly is larger than life.

So I get to the Rose Bowl itself, and there's such a great atmosphere, such a neat energy in the air. The stadium was exactly how I had pictured it, maybe even better. My seat was great, almost on the fifty-yard line. Ohio State played as well as it had all season and won what turned out to be a great game.

And then, there was that surreal moment that nothing could have prepared me for.

Late in the third quarter, in a matter of moments, the sun started setting beyond the San Gabriel Mountains outside the stadium. Suddenly, the mountains were absolutely radiant, glowing a golden glow that no artist could ever duplicate with a paint brush, a glow that no amount of high definition could translate to a television audience.

The world stopped. It was as if all ninety-five thousand fans noticed it at the same time. We all let out a collective gasp as we viewed one of the most breathtaking sights of our lifetime. The game itself became secondary for those next few prized moments as we all stared with awe at God's handiwork, nature's beauty. It was truly a spiritual experience.

And then it was gone, and suddenly, it was dark and the focus turned back to the game itself.

Today, I can look back at that golden moment and try to apply it to my everyday life. I had gone to Pasadena expecting to be wowed by bands and floats and roses. Didn't happen. Instead, I experienced something far more magnificent, something that seemingly came out of nowhere to take all our breaths away.

The program teaches us that what God has in store for us is far better than what we think we want for ourselves. The program teaches us that when we least expect it, God is there, and He is twenty thousand steps ahead of us, and we experience moments of pure joy.

I am struggling with some things these days for sure. I have a very uncertain future, and I don't know exactly what road I want my journey to take. I feel that my faith is strong, and that things will turn out exactly the way they're supposed to, so that's comforting.

But it's good to have reminders like that precious moment in Pasadena. Grateful am I.

BETTER TO COMFORT THAN TO BE COMFORTED

One of my very best friends relapsed recently.

I am still shocked, saddened, confused, and a thousand other emotions right now, because I absolutely did not see this coming, and I don't think anyone else did either. I hurt for this friend, because I know how much she is hurting and how much those near and dear to her are hurting.

So there is a lot of soul-searching going on, along with a commitment to be as encouraging and supportive as possible. The Serenity Prayer is paramount. Accept the things I cannot change. Do the things I can. And hopefully get the wisdom know the difference.

Already, I am finding that I will view relapses differently from this day forward.

You see, the "old-timer" in me has always taken a hard-line view of relapses. It takes what it takes. Rarely have we seen a person fail who has thoroughly followed our path. Everyone has their own personal bottom, and everyone must hit it before true recovery begins. Everything happens for a reason. If you relapse, there's some step you haven't fully taken—the first step obviously, but most definitely the third step and probably others too. A grateful alcoholic never drinks, so get some gratitude.

To be honest, I have gotten frustrated with most relapsers I have known, especially some of the chronic relapsers. I have often written them off, saying that when they are finally willing to go to any lengths to get sober, that's when they'll get sober. When they fully accept that drinking can no longer be an option under any circumstances, and accept that it's all about turning your will and life over to a higher power, that's when the promises will start coming true.

But now this.

There is no place for being a hard-liner right now. There is no place for trying to hammer home all the lessons that are supposed to be learned. There is no place for being judgmental. There is no place for any negativity. There is only a place for expressing unconditional love and 100 percent support and doing everything in my power to comfort and encourage and be a positive influence.

And—voila, it just hit me—if I can be that way for one of my best friends, I can be that way for every relapser. I may not hurt for everyone as much as I hurt for my friend right now, but I can put the tough love stuff on the side burner and do all the things that the eleventh-step prayer talks about. Better to comfort than to be comforted. Better to love than to be loved.

The truth is, when I came into the program, totally broken, scared as hell, full of regret and shame, and not sure if I could stay sober or not, I was showered with love. Everyone made me feel special. Everyone gave me hope. Everyone assured me it was going to be all right. There was nobody hammering away that I had to do this or I had to do that. There were no ultimatums, no scare tactics. They just showered me with love.

It's exactly what I needed at the time.

If that's exactly what I needed, then chances are it's exactly what relapsers and newcomers and everyone else who is struggling right now probably needs. That's the lesson I learn from all this. Yes, I've always tried to reach out to newcomers. I've always tried to congratulate relapsers when they pick up another white chip, maybe talk to them a little. But now, for sure, I'll try to do it with a lot more compassion.

That's what the program is all about.

I have been so fortunate in my lifetime to visit many of the greatest cities around the world and to attend just about every major sporting event, from Super Bowls to Wimbledon to the Masters to Final Fours and NBA Finals.

I've stood at midcourt in Madison Square Garden and Cameron Indoor Stadium, I've teed it up on the Old Course at St. Andrews, I've grabbed a handful of the frozen tundra at Lambeau Field on a day when it really was frozen, I've followed my beloved Buckeyes to the Rose Bowl, and I've stood along the Champs Elysees to cheer on the cyclists in the Tour de France.

For that matter, I've seen Clapton in Royal Albert Hall, Graham Nash at the Fillmore, the Eagles in Los Angeles on New Year's Eve Y2K, on and on and on.

Time after time, I have been filled with awe and joy and gratitude, and I've been overcome by the thought, "There's no place in the world I would rather be than right here, right now." What a fabulous feeling. To be totally at peace and filled with joy and gratitude and excitement, knowing that I was experiencing a moment that couldn't be topped.

But not so much over the last few years, even as these marvelous trips have continued. These days I suffer from depression, as much as I hate to admit it, as much as I don't want to. There are days I can't muster up any joy no matter what the occasion. Yes, I am on medication, but it seems to level me out, not allow me true joy. There are times when I should be happy, when I want to be happy, but it just doesn't happen.

Which brings me to a couple of weeks ago and a trip to San Francisco for Ohio State's game at California.

I had planned the trip last spring, and I had looked forward to it because, like I say, there is no place I'd rather be than at an Ohio State football game in the fall. The biggest days of the year to me are my sobriety date, Thanksgiving, Christmas, New Year's Day, my birthday, and the twelve Ohio State football Saturdays.

The hope, of course, was that I would feel all those great emotions on the trip, that the blahs would disappear long enough for me to enjoy a fantastic weekend in a city I loved, watching the team that I loved, having a blast as a fan instead of as a sportswriter or tour guide on the job.

I can't say it started off that well. Flight delays, packed into the planes like sardines, and a book I took along, *Proof of Heaven*, left me more confused and out of sorts than inspired. Yes, I was excited down deep to be going on the trip, but even with that the real joy was not surfacing the way I'd wished. Then I didn't sleep well, and that got me off on the wrong foot the next day, and I was tired, and I was this and that and not bad but not great—kind of like always.

Fortunately, it did change eventually, and the miracle is not that it changed, but how it changed.

I was at Ohio State's pregame pep rally, along with thousands of other Ohio State fans, and the band was about to start playing all the songs that are so dear to Ohioans—"Buckeye Battle Cry," "Across the Field," "Carmen Ohio," "Hang on Sloopy." It's *exactly* the scenario that has brought me so much joy in the past. And I wanted desperately to feel those emotions again, then and there.

So as the band marched in, I closed my eyes and said a prayer. I thanked God for allowing me to be at the pep rally, to be at the game, to be in San Francisco, thanks to jobs (and frequent flyer miles) that allowed me to make such trips. I thanked Him for a beautiful fall afternoon. I thanked Him for my Ohio heritage and a few other pertinent blessings. And then I asked, "Please, dear God, will you allow me to feel the joy inside me that I want to feel today? Will you please allow me to experience joy and happiness the way I have on these occasions throughout most of my life?"

The band started to play.

And suddenly, I was overcome with the strongest emotions that I could have ever asked for. I was full of joy. I was full of happiness and gratitude and a feeling that, yes, there was no place in the world that I would rather be than right there right then. I sat there amazed by it all, that I could be filled with joy so quickly, so fully. It turned into the neatest pep rally I have ever been to and then that carried on over to the game, and Ohio State won handily, and it carried on throughout the rest of the weekend. The next day, I sat in a Starbucks in Sausalito overlooking San Francisco Bay and watching the America's Cup race, and the very same emotions hit me. There's no place in the world I would rather be than right here, right now.

The awe-inspiring part is that I asked God for a day of joy and happiness, and He delivered almost instantaneously, far beyond anything I could have envisioned. He gave me a special weekend, and He allowed me to enjoy it to the fullest.

It was a perfect reminder that I can draw strength and joy and happiness through prayer, and that prayers do get answered, and that God is always with me. Now, I'm not sure I can summon up total joy on demand at all times—depression is too complicated and too wicked for that—but it sure is nice to know that it can happen at times, and that God is always there and His grace is most definitely available. It sure is nice to know that I can still be full of peace and joy and happiness.

It was an experience that will stick with me forever. I don't pray for the winning lottery numbers or make other equally outrageous requests of God, but I will have no problem asking him for the really important stuff in the future. I've always been true to the eleventh step, which in part says, "Praying only for knowledge of His will for us and the power to carry it out," and I will continue to be true to it for the most part. But now I'm mindful, too, of "Ask and ye shall receive."

What I received in San Francisco, most certainly, was a gift from God. I am so grateful.

I went to the retirement party for a friend over the weekend and saw my old boss for the first time in a while.

As we talked, I realized it wasn't just one of the highlights of the day—it was the perfect fodder for a sobriety blog.

All the things I now strive to be as a recovering alcoholic, my boss has always been blessed with naturally. He lives a 12-step program without even being in a 12-step program, abides by the principles that sometimes take recovering alcoholics an entire lifetime to grasp.

He is the very best I've ever seen at putting the past in the past and not holding a grudge. Once he has diffused a situation, it is over and done with, and he is on to the next task at hand. He has never had a vindictive bone in his body. I had more than one angry moment with him over the years, complaining about a bad headline or a chopped story or whatever, and he would always say his peace and then drop it. And in the heat of battle, he never took things too personally.

We alcoholics are the world's worst at that. We plot revenge. We harbor resentments. We dwell in the past to the point that it ruins the present and sometimes the future. Thankfully we're taught in the program how important it is to get rid of resentments, to live in the moment, to—as the Serenity Prayer says—accept the things we cannot change. But the truth is it doesn't come naturally, and sometimes it seems downright impossible. That's all in our alcoholic DNA.

Another thing my old boss is great at is looking for the best in every person. That's certainly not in my DNA, either. I'm a journalist, which means I'm cynical, I'm judgmental, I'm outspoken, I'm supposed to uncover all the bad and then expose everyone as phonies. And the alcoholic in me was always on the lookout for people trying to get me, assuming the worst, in whatever the situation would be. Not too proud of that these days. But there my boss was at the party, telling old stories and saying nice things about people I had only negative memories of. It gave me a lot to think about.

The Big Book is pretty clear about it—if you focus on the negative, the problem gets bigger. If you focus on the positive, the solution gets bigger. If you look for a person's strengths, you come away with a completely different picture than if you look for their weaknesses. But we alcoholics don't always remember that.

Got to tell you about a conversation with his wife too. Their daughter had gone off to college, and she made a conscious, corporate decision before she ever got to school that she was not going to drink. Ever. For four years. She had seen all the damage that others her age had done to themselves, all the heartache it produced, and she was determined not to let any of that happen to her. She has had to stand up to peer pressure during her college years, and no doubt it hasn't always been easy. But she's a true success, and she's going to be (or already is) just like her parents.

So there are people out there who do it the right way, who are well-adjusted, who understand the meaning of life and reap all the rewards of living the right way. I'm lucky to have worked for one. My only question is, why didn't I try to follow his lead better years and years ago?

The only way I can come remotely close to living a proper and prosperous life today is by trying to work the steps. And even when I'm doing my best, which hasn't always been the case, it's not easy. The beauty of the 12-step program is that it gives us ideals to shoot for and it gives us the tools to use that normal people seem to have been born with. Thank God the steps exist. I am lost without them.

MY PRICELESS ARTWORK FROM KLAUS VOORMANN

It might be worth the $700 I paid for it.

It might be worth more than that, maybe even several thousand dollars.

Or it might not be worth much more than the paper it's printed on.

Whatever, it's priceless to me, and it is one of the neatest things that has ever happened to me. There's a life lesson involved, to boot.

A while back, I commissioned rock icon Klaus Voormann to do a piece of artwork for me that would complement all the John Lennon artwork I have accumulated.

This is the same Klaus Voormann who was responsible for the cover on the Beatles' *Revolver* album, the same Klaus Voormann who befriended the Beatles early on during their Hamburg days and who went on to play bass for several bands, including Lennon's Plastic Ono Band.

We kicked around some ideas and wound up with a piece that has been named "Abbey Feet." It's a pencil drawing in Klaus's classic style with the Beatles crossing the street as they did on the "Abbey Road" album, only this piece of artwork cuts them off at the waist and just focuses in on their feet and the famous crosswalk markings.

There's John leading the way in his tennis shoes, followed by Ringo in his boots, a barefoot Paul—with his hand and a cigarette falling down into the picture—and finally George in boots as well.

It's not only signed by Klaus, but he also was gracious enough to enclose a personalized handwritten note that expressed how happy he was to add to my collection.

The thing that means the most is that it's a totally unique, one-of-a-kind piece of artwork that came directly from Klaus himself. Not a poster bought on a website or a limited-edition print of three hundred or the like. It's a totally unique, commissioned piece. From one of John's best friends, from the guy who made rock art history by designing the *Revolver* cover.

How this all unfolded is just as special.

I was having trouble sleeping one night, and after enough tossing and turning, I decided to get up and get on the internet.

I was just typing in any .com I could think of. I remember going to StephenStills.com and NeilYoung.com and various other musicians, just to see what kind of website might pop up.

For whatever reason, I don't know why, I typed in KlausVoormann.com.

It was his website, for sure, and there was a picture of him and a message on the home page. He said he was totally retired these days and was concentrating more on his artwork than his music. He said if anyone ever wanted a piece of artwork, to go ahead and email him.

I took the bait immediately and sent an email, explaining that I was not a Beatles memorabilia collector or anything but that I owned eleven pieces of John's artwork, some limited-edition serigraphs that included John's trademark line drawings and also several cartoon-style drawings John did for his son Sean. I asked if Klaus would be interested in coming up with something that could complement those serigraphs.

He replied by saying he loved the idea, and he would love to add to my collection.

We agreed on a dollar figure, and from there, it was totally his vision on what he wanted to come up with.

A couple of weeks later, it came in the mail, direct from Munich, Germany, and then it was just a matter of getting it framed and getting it mounted on the wall.

It wound up being more spectacular than I ever could have imagined.

What I marvel at is that I grew up loving the Beatles, but never in a million years could I imagine that one day I would be commissioning a piece of artwork from the same guy who designed the *Revolver* cover, which is definitely one of the most iconic album covers in rock music history. Never in a million years could I imagine that I would ever even have contact with someone like Klaus, let alone get a personalized note wishing me peace and love.

In my career as a sportswriter, I have had interactions with some of the greatest athletes in history, and that has never fazed me. But to deal with Klaus Voormann—well, that's through the roof.

The life lesson is that anything's possible, and sometimes God can be giving you something beyond your wildest dreams.

If I'd fallen asleep on time that night, none of this would have happened. If I hadn't emailed him that night, none of this would have happened. And everything else just fell into place after that.

Interestingly, if you go to Klaus's website now, the home page is gone, and there is no way to make direct contact with him, so I was truly in the right place at the right time.

Grateful I am. Thank you, God. Thank you, Klaus. And to everyone else, the piece is always on display anytime you want to see it.

OUR WHOLE ATTITUDE AND OUTLOOK UPON LIFE WILL CHANGE

I heard my sister scream.

When I ran down the stairs, I saw my mother lying on the floor, in a pool of blood, unable to move.

She had slipped on one of the last steps leading to the basement of my house. She had taken a head-first crash into one of the bookshelves, then hit hard on the concrete floor.

A 911 call was made. The medics came quickly and got her to the emergency room, and there doctors determined that she had a broken wrist, a broken shoulder, and would of course require several stitches to patch up the gash above her eye.

My immediate reaction to the doctors' report?

I was relieved. I was grateful that she hadn't broken her hip, which would have been devastating and permanently life-changing for an eighty-four-year-old even in the good physical and mental shape that she is in. I was grateful that everything that happened to her was fixable, even if it was going to require surgeries and a lot of discomfort and a long road of rehabilitation.

I'm not sure, but I think that's the way normal people react. Thank goodness it wasn't worse. Thank goodness it will all be okay.

What I have come to realize in the time since is that my immediate reaction, which seemed to come automatically, was a sign of the program working in my life. It was indeed a gift of the program.

Alcoholics don't usually react to tragedy or adversity the way normal people react. We're predispositioned to focus on the negative, to take the glass-is-half-empty view. An active alcoholic would be angry that anything happened in the first place, angry at God for letting it happen, certainly unable to thank God that it wasn't worse.

I can tell you, there was a time in my life when I thought this "Thank goodness it wasn't worse" stuff was a bunch of Pollyanna crap. There was a time in my life, even long after I got sober, when I would have said this was really, really bad, period, and there was nothing good that could possibly come out of it.

Where the beauty of the program comes in, in the bigger picture, is gratitude.

We recovering alcoholics have to recondition our minds to be grateful instead of resentful. We have to look at the glass as half full instead of half empty, or else we will never have any significant amount of serenity. We have to accept the things we cannot change, like a nasty fall down the stairs by a loved one, and we have to have the courage to change our reaction to it. And then we have to get into action mode and live it, not just talk it.

This gift of a new outlook has filtered into other areas of my life. A few years back, I was laid off from a great job I'd had for twenty-one years. Yes, there was some sadness and self-pity, and a feeling that it had all been for nothing. But for the most part, I was able to rise above that and just be grateful for all the opportunities I had had during those twenty-one years. I was an NBA beat writer for fourteen years, traveling the country and covering games nine months out of the year. I covered preseason NBA games in Paris and Bologna, Italy, for crying out loud. I covered Super Bowls, the Masters, US Open tennis and golf, and the list goes on and on. All things that had made my career better than my wildest dreams.

My sports editor could vouch that there were plenty of times I wasn't grateful, that I felt a sense of entitlement. But I can honestly say that today I look back at all those years and all those opportunities as blessings, and I am extremely grateful.

My current job has its unique challenges and frustrations. But when I get the most frustrated, I remind myself that the good far outweighs the bad and, hey, I've got a job.

A change in thinking, indeed. That's one of *The Big Book*'s promises. Our whole attitude and outlook upon life will change.

And the neat thing is, I now have gratitude as a weapon against whatever befalls me. I have gratitude as a tool in the toolbox for coping with any curve balls that life presents. If I get out of whack emotionally, I have the ability to refocus on the positives in my life. I know to focus on the solution, not the problem. And for sure, thanks to the program, I have a sponsor and friends in recovery who can remind me of all this if and when I forget.

Now for the best part. My mom's surgeries were successful, she is doing wonderfully, and she is far ahead of schedule in terms of rehabilitation. She's got a trip to Scotland to look forward to in April, and she's intent on going. She was able to use her experience and hope to help another woman I know who took a similar spill on the ice recently, who also broke her shoulder.

It's all good. It really is.

THE LITTLE PRINCESS AND THE REWARDS OF GIVING BACK

We call her Little Princess, because she is so special.

She is an African American woman now in her early thirties, and when I say African American, it is in the truest sense. She was born and raised in Liberia and moved to the United States at age eleven.

She can light up a room with her bright smile and constant cheer. She is one of the most gregarious, refreshing, positive people I have ever known. You can't help but smile when you're around her. She is precious, and she is inspirational.

At a meeting the other night, a fellow alcoholic introduced her to the group as the personification of "happy, joyous, and free," and I agree wholeheartedly.

I first got to know her about six years ago, when she was new to the program and wasn't anywhere near so upbeat. She had clearly had enough of drinking, was clearly hurting, was in desperate need of turning her life around. She had hit her own personal bottom and needed help badly—and quickly.

It so happened that about the same time, there were five or six others who were about her same age coming into the program and all going to the same meeting. They instantly hit it off and banded together, to go through the steps and the early stages of sobriety as a group.

What happened in their first year of sobriety was probably the most-amazing phenomenon I have ever seen in recovery. They all latched onto the program with passion, and it clicked instantly. They grew and grew and grew, all six or seven of them, and in doing so they rejuvenated every other member of the group. They went through all the highs and lows together, leaning on each other during the tough times and sharing their joy during the good times, and they carried the bond beyond the meeting rooms and into their daily lives. They became friends forever.

It's rare when you see two or three people come into the program at the same time who all get it. And yet this was six or seven, all on fire. It was a sight to behold.

So fast forward to a couple of summers ago, long after various folks had gone various directions, some moving out of town.

It was Father's Day, and out of the clear blue, I got a text message on my phone. It was from Little Princess. And her words just blew me away.

She was writing to wish me a Happy Father's Day. She was writing to thank me for all the support and guidance I had always given her over the years. She said that I had done more for her than her own father, and she wanted me to know how much she appreciated it.

More than her own father? Wow. My first reaction was sadness that she didn't have a better relationship with her father. But then I quickly started to realize that I had just been given the greatest compliment of my entire lifetime.

I'm single. I don't have any children. It is the greatest disappointment and failure of my life. And yet here was somebody saying I'd had a bigger impact on them than their own father, wishing me a Happy Father's Day. Totally unexpected, totally unsolicited. I am humbled beyond description. It is a moment in time I will never forget, and it will continue to make future Father's Days all the more special.

The truth is all I have ever done is pass on what was so freely given to me in the program. All I have ever done is offer my experience, strength, and hope, just like millions of other recovering alcoholics have done with newcomers around the world. Certainly I've taken an interest in Little Princess and the others, and I've always cared for them all and supported them all. But the pleasure has been all mine because it has been so neat to see them all grow and embrace the program the way they have. I was hardly the only member of the group to give them support. Everyone reached out to them, and everyone was supportive.

I guess the lesson I take out of this is that you just never know how much of an impact you might have on a newcomer if you just do your job and carry the message. Suit up and show up, and let God take over from there.

It so happens that two others in that group of six or seven wound up asking me to sponsor them. It has been just as joyous to see them work the program and grow and grow and to see them get all the benefits that the program has to offer.

I didn't sponsor anyone during my first twenty years or so in the program. At first I was too new to the program, then I moved, then I went through years where I was only going to about ten meetings a year and staying sober on the first three steps alone. Hard to sponsor someone if you're not going to meetings.

These last seven or eight years sponsoring various newcomers have been golden though. I have learned how vitally important it is to work the twelfth step and give back, not just take. We say in recovery that you have to give it away to keep it, and what I have found is that by giving it away I have received much more in return than I could have dreamed of. I have tried to create a family atmosphere and stress the fellowship of it all, because that's what my original sponsor and his wife did when I was a newcomer. My sponsees are like sons, and Little Princess, well, obviously she's pretty special too.

As *The Big Book* says, it works. It really does.

THE BEST WAY POSSIBLE TO GET
THE BEST DEAL POSSIBLE

My dad always said that the day he died would be the greatest day of his life.

Not that he was ready for it to end, because nobody loved life more than him. It's just that because of a couple of specific spiritual experiences in his life he was sure there was an afterlife, and he was certain that he was going to heaven.

So when he died back in 2002, I felt a million emotions that I'd never felt before. Mostly grief and sadness, obviously, but in the back of my mind was this notion that he was indeed living on.

I privately hoped that someday, somehow, he would make it clear to me that he was all right and that everything he had believed was right on the money. I didn't know if it would come in the form of a dream, or a vision, or exactly what, I just hoped something definitively would happen.

Years passed. I never felt it, as much as I wanted to. It actually surprised me that nothing had happened, because down deep I really did think that somehow, someday he would give me some sort of sign.

So it came time to buy a new car.

Let me back track a second and say that he was the world's greatest car shopper. He would go from dealership to dealership, comparing, bartering, playing one against the other, getting this accessory added or that discount added or a little extra on his trade-in. When he bought a car, you could be certain that he had gotten the absolute best deal possible.

I, on the other hand, have always been the exact opposite. I've been taken to the cleaners more than once in my lifetime. There was the yellow AMC Pacer straight out of college that truly was a lemon. I had a Pontiac Fiero that blew not one but two engines. Once I went into a dealership stressing that I couldn't wind up with payments of more than $250 a month, being assured by the salesman that they wouldn't be more than $250. By the time they added everything up, my payments were $330 something. And they'd already sold my trade-in, so I couldn't back out of the deal.

My dad had actually helped me with my previous purchase, and I got a good deal. He did all the haggling and all I had to do was drive my old car to Florida, sign the papers, and drive the new car back home.

But now I was on my own again. I dreaded the whole ordeal. I was convinced that I would get taken to the cleaners again, just like always. I had no confidence in myself as far as bartering, and I feared the worst.

A local dealership was running a television commercial with what I thought were great lease rates for the exact make and model I had been thinking about. I went to the dealership, and sure enough, they said they had sold out of the makes and models that were being advertised. They could offer a different model at a significantly higher rate, beyond what I was hoping to spend. So this thing was starting out exactly the way so many previous car shopping expeditions had.

With their offer in hand, I decided to go to another dealership to compare, to see if they could give me a lease better than what I had just been offered. They couldn't or wouldn't. And so here I was back at square one, again disillusioned by the entire process.

The more I thought about it, the more ticked off I got that the first dealership was still running television ads about prices they weren't honoring. I got online and wrote an email to the manager to complain. I made it clear that I had been very happy with my previous car, wanted to do business with them, but just felt that a bait-and-switch was going on.

He invited me back to the dealership, apologized, and said that he would be committed to giving me the best deal possible.

The back-and-forth didn't stop there, obviously. But to make a long story short, eventually they offered me a lease of an upgraded model, at the same price they were advertising originally. Then they went another step farther. Rather than lease it, they said, what if I bought it? I looked at the payments and the bottom line, and it was way, way better than anything I could have imagined. I was floored that everything had fallen into place the way it did and that I was getting what I felt was a great deal.

So I wound up buying the car, a Honda CRV.

Driving home, relieved to say the least and very pleased with the way it had all unfolded, I was overcome by one thought. No question about it, my dad had been with me throughout the process. His spirit had guided me through the whole ordeal, and there I was, just like him, getting the best deal possible. It was the first time since his death that I felt that yes, he was there with me, that yes, he was in fact living on.

That Honda CRV just surpassed two hundred thousand miles, and it is still going strong. It has never had any major problems, knock on wood. It has long been paid off. It still looks almost new. I couldn't be happier with it or more grateful for it.

Now, of course, I'm greedy. I want to be filled with his spirit all the time, not just when I go car shopping. He loved people, and he had such a gift to be able to put people at ease, and to make them smile, and to look for the good in everyone. I've never been that way. I'm an old newspaperman, a cynic, and as a recovering alcoholic I'm always wary of people out to hurt me. I wish I was more optimistic and good-hearted like him.

In the program, we talk about drawing strength from God and about God doing for us what we could not do for ourselves. *The Big Book* says that deep down within us is the fundamental concept of God, and it is only there that it can be found.

I still don't grasp that totally. But obviously in this one case, I was able to tap into that power, to draw the strength to negotiate the best deal possible, just like my dad always had. I still have a great car to show for us. And lessons learned, of course.

GOING BACK TO PARIS, *C'EST MAGNIFIQUE!*

I am heading back to Paris for the umpteenth time later this week for the French Open, and the excitement is building because to me, Paris is the greatest city in the world.

I say umpteenth because it could be my thirteenth or sixteenth or maybe more than that. I've lost count.

This is all a tribute to sobriety, and I am so, so grateful, because before sobriety, the notion that I would ever make it to Europe even once was totally absurd.

Before sobriety, I was bouncing checks on Wednesday to buy my liquor until payday Friday, living paycheck to paycheck. All my credit cards were cut off. I was living in a dump of an apartment that had liquor bottles, record albums, and old pizza boxes strewn everywhere; the sink always full of dirty dishes. I was a mess physically, emotionally, morally, and spiritually. I traveled some, to be sure, because of my job as a sportswriter, but my drinking was putting my job in serious jeopardy because of all the embarrassing and idiotic things I had done when drunk.

Sixteen trips to Paris in my future? Yeah, right.

Anyway, I now cherish each trip and try to turn each into its own little spiritual journey. I take an attitude of gratitude with me—how can anyone go to Paris and not pinch themselves in awe?—and each time I'm there, I am very cognizant of how far sobriety has brought me.

Some of the biggest highlights of each trip now are the meetings and reconnecting with friends in the program I have met there over the years. The noon meeting at the American Cathedral has become my home-away-from-home group of sorts over the years. It's a mix of expats living in Paris, American tourists, and native Parisians who say the English-speaking meetings are better than the French-speaking meetings. So you have a diverse group of folks who are there absolutely because they *want* to be there.

Over the years, I have seen the program work its magic in many forms in Paris. I listened to a fifth step once because the guy wanted to do his fifth step totally anonymously with an American tourist, someone he'd never see again. Another time I was able to help a newcomer get involved more deeply with the program, because he was able to open up after he heard where I was from—a city he had lived in years before. Now he's a real stalwart in Paris AA.

I have heard some profound shares, including one that will stick with me forever. It was a meeting on the second step: came to believe that a power greater than ourselves could restore us to sanity. The woman was talking about her relationship with her higher power and how it had evolved and continued to evolve. She said at some point she came to an eye-opening realization.

"My conscience is not my God," she said. "God is my God."

Boom. Did that ever hit me. I had grown up with the notion that God was in fact manifested in my conscience. If my conscience told me something, it was God telling me right from wrong. But see, something happened during those years of drinking. My conscience got totally warped. It either justified everything or beat me up unmercifully for all the things I did or didn't do. And then after I got sober, it turned into a very, very punitive entity. I learned in the program to forgive others, but my conscience wouldn't allow me to forgive myself. As a result, I continued to beat myself up over years, the big stuff for sure, but also the most trivial stuff.

"My conscience is not my God. God is my God."

What an epiphany. When I heard that and fully grasped it and applied it to my life, I was finally able to separate the two. Yes, my conscience will beat me up sometimes. But no, that's not God beating me up. God's love is unconditional. The beating up is more likely the disease trying to be cunning, baffling, and powerful.

I'm not going to say I don't listen to my conscience anymore, but I will say that I am more likely to listen to my heart instead. I let God lead me through my heart, not through a bombardment of negativity. And what I find is that I am much happier and at peace because of it.

So now I head back to Paris, full of gratitude and curiosity. Who knows what God's got in store this time?

PARIS, PICKPOCKETS, AND A
SPIRITUAL JOURNEY

This summer has been filled with international travel—first a week in Paris in May, followed by sixteen days in London, Edinburgh, Paris, and Brussels at the end of June and early July.

Funny how one incident can change everything.

On my first day in Paris on the first trip, I had my wallet pickpocketed. Was on the Metro, was aware that pickpockets are rampant on the Metro, was only going a couple of stops, let my guard down for just a second…and voila, the next thing I knew, my wallet was gone.

I didn't know if I was going to cry or throw up. I wanted to do both.

It was a feeling I have never experienced—a total sense of violation and fear and anger (at myself, for letting it happen) and despair and, most of all, loneliness.

I can honestly say that I have never felt lonelier in my entire life.

I remember sitting in my hotel room trying to sort it all out, wondering how I was going to cope and how I was going to survive and do my job for the rest of the week.

I said a few prayers and leaned on God as much as I could, and eventually, I was overcome with one very spiritual notion. No, I didn't have any money or credit cards. But I had my relationship with God. I had my sobriety. I had my family. I had my health. I had a very select few friends that were always going to be there in good times and bad. I had my soul, pierced as it was at that particular moment.

I still had all the things that really mattered.

Of course, I got through it. Two days later, I ran into a friend at the French Open who loaned me one hundred euros and that got me through the rest of the week. I made a meeting at the American Cathedral, saw some old familiar faces there, and that helped. Eventually good old "this too shall pass" became a reality, and all I was really out of was some money.

There was a moment, I admit, where I asked God, "Why did you let this happen to me?" But even as I was saying it, there was the realization that I was going down the wrong path with that kind of thinking.

I may never look at a European trip the same again. I noticed on my return trip that I was constantly on guard, especially on the London Tube and Paris Metro, maybe to the point of not being able to fully enjoy the trip as I had for trip after trip in the past. Something was definitely different.

But it was still good for me to go through it all, to realize that money is great, but it is just money, to realize that the really important things in life are God, sobriety, family, health, and friends. Fortunately, I still have them all.

IT'S A FAMILY DISEASE, MORE THAN I EVER REALIZED

There is no alcoholism in my immediate family, except for me.

My parents never drank. I've never known my sister to drink. My brother will share a bottle of wine with his wife from time to time but can basically take it or leave it. He got into a little trouble one night with a bunch of buddies while in college and said to heck with that if it's going to cause problems.

So I can't blame my alcoholism on genetics. I have no one to blame but myself. From the time I was young, I couldn't wait until I was old enough to drink, and once I started drinking, I loved it, and I drank my way through college. Then once I got out on my own, I drank and drank and drank, and eventually, I crossed over that invisible line into alcoholism.

That means I'm not like so many alcoholics who were raised by alcoholics or surrounded by alcoholism growing up. I only saw the glamorous side of drinking; I never experienced all the fear and shame and anger that is inherent in a dysfunctional alcoholic family environment. Even after I got into recovery, I had no real experience with or appreciation of how negatively impacted an entire family can be by this disease.

But for the past year or so, I have seen this phenomenon first-hand, up close and personal. I have seen the wicked and devastating impact that the disease can have on innocent, caring, loving family members who have done nothing to deserve their fate. I have seen firsthand how an alcoholic can bring everyone down with him, in line with what *The Big Book* says about the alcoholic being like a tornado ripping through the lives of others.

One of my best friends has a son who is in the throes of active alcoholism. The son has been in and out of treatment centers countless times. He has followed a predictable pattern, drinking himself into oblivion and then routinely winding up in detox, but only after going underground and shutting himself off from everyone else for extended, mysterious stretches.

He has gone to the 12-step program but says that he hates it, that it's not for him. And so he lives the life of denial, thinking that this is the time he'll be able to manage it better, that he can do it on his own with the help of a psychiatrist and Antabuse, a drug which makes one violently sick when combined with alcohol. He apologizes over and over, swearing he won't drink again. He speaks of his shame as if it is some sort of justification for his actions. But this cycle continues time and again, and each time the episodes and the suffering get worse, because after all, alcoholism is a progressive disease.

He is a classic, textbook practicing alcoholic, totally predictable, the absolute definition of insanity—doing the same thing over and over and hoping for different results.

We in recovery know the inevitable outcome of untreated alcoholism. Jails, institutions, or death. We know all about denial. We know the importance of hitting bottom, which is so necessary to provide the alcoholic with the gift of desperation. Most of all, we know that the 12-step program works if you work it, but never will if you don't.

So we reach out and offer to help and wait for the defining moment when he either starts the road to recovery or crashes and burns completely.

Meanwhile, the rest of the family lives a tortured existence. They helplessly watch someone they love go downhill farther and farther, and they know from doing their homework exactly where it is all headed. They worry about him night and day, so much that it becomes a constant cloud over all they do. They want desperately to be supportive and help in any way they can, but they also understand how powerless they are to do anything except pray and hope for the best.

They are both angry at him for refusing help and sympathetic toward him for being so sick, hurting every bit as much or even more so than he does. They anguish over where exactly the line is between loving unconditionally and enabling. Their emotions vary and sometimes what seemed like a good idea yesterday doesn't seem so good today. They pray, and yet the situation continues to get worse instead of better.

And they all have different personalities and different ways of coping with it all, so the variables multiply. Naturally, there are times when they second-guess themselves, times when there are disagreements among them. So they have bursts of frustration, and then the need for fence-mending within the ranks afterward.

Fortunately in this case, their deep faith has gotten them through the ordeal so far, or as well as could be expected. They are living by the serenity prayer, asking for the serenity to accept the things they cannot change, the courage to change the things they can, and the wisdom to know the difference.

But it is a day to day, hour to hour, minute to minute struggle for everyone.

I will never know how much I put my family through during my drinking years, especially in the final days. Fortunately, they lived five hundred miles away, so they couldn't have known just how bad the situation really was. They got the late-night telephone calls when I was hammered and depressed, and they had to bail me out financially at times because I was in so much debt, and clearly, intuition told them there was something terribly wrong. But I hope it didn't engulf their lives morning, noon, and night.

So this has been an eye-opening experience for me. I have compassion for the family in a way I have never had compassion before. More compassion for the family than for the son, to be honest. I am able to guide them a bit, although I feel vastly inadequate as an adviser, and I am able to answer their questions from a recovering alcoholic's standpoint. I feel good knowing that I can sometimes offer comfort, or a little bit of sanity, to the situation. The St. Francis prayer says it's better to comfort than be comforted, and I definitely feel that as I try to help.

It's a desperate situation though. This disease is cunning, baffling, and powerful, as *The Big Book* says. It is also, clearly, a disease that impacts the entire family.

MY HOUSE IS A VERY, VERY, VERY FINE HOUSE

As Crosby, Stills, and Nash would sing, my house is a very, very, very fine house.

It's the nicest house I've ever lived in, and it truly is my dream home. Neat porch in front overlooking a golf course and lake. Huge deck in the back that leads to trees full of birds, squirrels, and sometimes even a few deer. Great neighborhood, great neighbors. A very contemporary look and floor plan. More room than I really need, although it's nice having the extra space. Somehow, all the furniture and artwork I've accumulated in the past thirty years seems to blend together perfectly.

I hope I can stay there for the rest of my life.

I bring it up because recently I celebrated eight years in it, and it has caused moments of reflection.

I can remember during my drinking years when I used to live in a rathole apartment, with a mattress on the floor in the tiny bedroom, dishes stacked up in the kitchen sink, pizza boxes and liquor bottles strewn everywhere, record albums scattered all across the living room. The rent was only like $275 a month, and I still couldn't pay on time, because I was living paycheck to paycheck and bouncing checks on Wednesday to get enough liquor to make it to payday on Friday.

Back then, the notion that I would one day be living in an ultra-modern 3,900-square-foot house on the golf course would have been totally ludicrous.

So I look at my house as a blessing, as a sign of how far I've come over the years thanks to sobriety, as a symbol of who I am today and what I will continue to try to be in the future. It is truly a home, not just a place to live, and I am so grateful for it.

More than that, though, my house represents a couple of great lessons that I always need to remember.

The first came from my aunt. It was before I bought the house, at a time when I was debating whether to buy it or remain where I was living in a nearby neighborhood. I was in a huge quandary, not sure what to do. On one hand, this house was more house than I really needed, the cost was more than I ever dreamed of paying for any house, and the mortgage would have been right on the border-line of what I could afford monthly. On the other hand, I absolutely *loved* the house. It was everything I ever wanted in a house. It had the look and feel that was absolutely me. And while the price tag was high, it was in a popular, growing area where property values would surely go up.

I remember all the internal debates. My heart was telling me to buy it, but my head was saying not to. One day I felt one way, the next day I would feel the other way. I prayed and prayed about it, hoping that God would give me the right answer in the form of a big neon sign that I couldn't misinterpret. I talked to others, got differing advice. I absolutely didn't know what I was going to do, or how it was all going to turn out.

In a conversation with my aunt, I mentioned precisely that— that I wished God would give me a big neon sign telling me to either buy the house or to drop the notion. Was it God's will that I buy the house, or was it God's will that I not buy the house?

Her answer was something I had not even considered. She said, "God doesn't care if you buy the house or not. He just wants you to be happy if you do, and be happy if you don't. So make a decision and then make the best of it."

That's a concept I have tried to apply to everything since. It cuts out the constant back-and-forth and indecision, and it gives me the assurance that if my motives are right, and I have done all the legwork, whatever decision I make will probably turn out all right.

Turns out I made a lowball offer, it was accepted, and that told me it was meant to be.

The second lesson comes straight from *The Big Book*. There's a paragraph just before the third-step prayer that talks about God and says: "Being all powerful, He provided what we needed, if we kept close to Him and performed His work well." Those are my marching orders, to stay close to God, which I do with prayer, and to perform His work well, which I take to mean helping others and going to meetings and working the steps and trying to walk like I talk.

My experience, in general and specifically with this house, is that He does, indeed, provide what we need.

I haven't missed a payment or even been late with a payment, despite going through a stretch where I was laid off from my job of twenty-one years. I haven't missed any meals, that's for sure. I haven't sunk into deep debt. And I love my house every bit as much today as I did eight years ago when I bought it.

All I've done in those eight years is try to stay close to God and perform His work well, just like *The Big Book* says.

And each morning, I thank Him for a great place to live.

HOW GOD TURNED ME INTO A TENNIS WRITER

We talk in the program about the mosaic of our lives, how one seemingly small event winds up leading to bigger and better things and winds up shaping our futures.

Only in retrospect can we see how God's plan all came to fruition, how He was ten thousand steps ahead of us all along with blessings far greater than we could have imagined.

For me, a great example is how I became a tennis writer.

I played tennis for fun, not seriously, while growing up. I enjoyed watching Wimbledon and the US Open because I was a sports fan, but I was hardly a die-hard tennis junkie.

When I became a sportswriter, there was continued interest, but for the first twenty years of my journalism career, I strictly covered golf, college and pro basketball, and college and pro football.

The newspaper I worked for had a lady who was a Hall of Fame sportswriter who had covered tennis for decades and was a legend in the city. So there was no need for me to cover any tennis, no expectation that I would ever need to.

The one thing I did each year was go to the US Open for a couple of days, but only as a fan, and as much to spend a weekend in New York as to spend all my time watching tennis.

So fast forward, and in 2001, it was announced that the city where I worked was going to host a Davis Cup match. It was only a relegation match, but it was a huge event in our city, and the biggest movers and shakers in our city were the ones behind it.

My newspaper decided to do it up really big and rightly so. There were plans to put out a special section leading up to the weekend, and then a four-page wrap of coverage daily.

The lady legend, well into her eighties by then, was starting to slow down at that point and couldn't produce all the copy that would need to be written. And she had no desire to travel to the US Open to do the advance work that needed to be done.

It was late August, early September, still a month away from when the NBA season would start back up. It was my normal down-time before the start of training camp.

So my sports editor asked, "Do you want to go to the US Open and write stories for the special section?"

Given the chance to spend a week in New York on the company's dime, I enthusiastically said yes.

So it all worked out well, and I accumulated plenty of material in New York, and then came home and wrote and wrote and wrote. The Davis Cup tie was initially postponed because of the 9-11 attacks (I flew home from New York the night of September 10, so I missed it all by about fourteen hours), but when it was finally played, it was a huge success.

It was fun to be a part of, thoroughly enjoyable, and I was satisfied that I had done a good job despite not being a real tennis junkie.

I figured that would be the end of my tennis writing career.

But the Davis Cup returned for another match in 2007, this time a far-bigger match with the United States against powerhouse Spain.

Again, I was summoned into action, and again I was excited to be a part of it all.

That weekend, too, went well, and our newspaper was getting huge praise from the local leaders, the USTA, and the players as well.

That weekend was so successful, in fact, that the Davis Cup returned again the following year, for another huge match against another powerhouse, France. Our newspaper continued to do it up big, and once again, it was a huge success and a lot of fun to be a part of.

I was convinced at that point that my days of writing tennis were over once and for all.

It seemed definite when I was eventually laid off after twenty-one years at the newspaper in 2010.

So I had a lot of good memories, and I was grateful that I'd had the experience to cover the Davis Cup ties and to have been a part of something special.

Here's where God entered the picture.

I was out of work, living off a severance package until it ran out, and the collecting unemployment and just picking up a few bucks here and there with freelance assignments.

And lo and behold, it was announced that the city had landed an annual ATP World Tour tournament, which was just a huge coup for the city. The same local leaders and movers and shakers who had been so kind to me during the Davis Cup matches were behind this tournament, and suddenly, a job opportunity opened up.

They wound up hiring me to write all their website stories and to write all the stories for the tournament program.

That was five years ago, and we're all still going strong as this year's tournament is set to begin.

I am amazed by it all—how it has all unfolded.

When I was at my lowest point, out of a job, not knowing what I was going to do with the rest of my life, no real exciting prospects on the horizon, the notion that the city would get a professional tennis tournament and that I would be a part of it would have seemed outrageous.

But that's exactly how it all happened.

When I desperately needed some kind of job, God dropped a great one in my lap, totally out of left field. And very, very importantly, the new income stream came just when I needed it most.

We talk in the program about how when one door closes another one opens. There is a paragraph in *The Big Book* that says that God will always provide what we need, as long as we stay close to Him and perform His work well.

This entire chapter in my life is proof positive.

Some people would call it all serendipity or mere chance. I choose to believe God had it all planned this way all along.

LESSONS LEARNED FROM BILL W.'S SWEDISH IVY

Not too long ago, a dear friend gave me a shoot from the famous Bill W. Swedish Ivy plant.

For those of you not familiar with the story, there was a Swedish Ivy plant in Bill's hospital room in Miami shortly before he died in 1971. Lois apparently took the plant back to Stepping Stones after Bill died, and she kept the plant for years. At some point, she pinched off one of the shoots, gave it to a friend, and a tradition was started. From that moment offshoots have been passed on and on throughout the recovery community.

Obviously, there is no way to confirm that my shoot is a direct descendant from the original, but I choose to believe it is, and even if it isn't, it's so symbolic of the program and how the program grows when we pass it on.

The shoot has grown and multiplied pretty quickly in the time I've had it and has looked really nice in the kitchen window. It reminds me of the program every time I look at it.

So then came last week, when I was gone for seven nights to the Masters.

I had no idea how much water a Swedish Ivy needed to survive—I'm a sportswriter, not a botanist or a gardener—so naturally, I wondered how it would look once I got home after seven days of no watering. Would it shrivel up and die, or would it be as strong as ever?

When I got home, the answer was apparent. It looked terrible. The leaves had indeed shriveled up, and while the plant was not dead, it sure wasn't full of much life. Let's say it was on life support.

I immediately watered it but wondered if it might be too little, too late.

Much to my surprise, the next morning, the plant looked better than ever, the leaves a deeper green than I had remembered them, the shoots strong and no longer drooping.

Didn't take me long to get a mini meeting and a blog topic out of the results.

This plant apparently is just like the 12-step program. If you don't water it, it dies quickly. But the beauty of it—the plant and the program—is that even if it shrivels up and starts to die, it doesn't take much to get it back to full strength, or even better than ever.

My sobriety has been that way for sure. I was all gung ho when I got sober, and I grew and grew spiritually and emotionally. Then came success and a better job and a move to another city, and suddenly, things started getting in the way, and the quality of my program definitely wilted. For years. But when I finally made the decision to jump full-bore back into the program, and started nurturing my relationship with God again, it didn't take long at all to get stronger than ever.

I would humbly say that my program has never been better than it has been for the last several years, and I am so grateful to be able to say that.

This is what I try to impart to others, too, particularly my sponsees. I have one sponsee who was absolutely on fire when he came into the program. It was so rewarding to see him embrace sobriety and work the program to the best of his ability and to see all the positive results. He's currently going through a lull in his sobriety, and I am trying to convince him that it's like riding a bicycle. If he gets back on the bike and starts pedaling again, he'll get to where he wants to be program-wise, spiritually and emotionally, in no time flat.

There's another lesson I get out of the Swedish Ivy.

In recovery, we talk about how we can start our day over at any point. No matter how bad a day starts out, we can always hit the default button and take a deep breath and say a prayer and start again. This is one of the tools in the toolbox, a way to cope with whatever adversity there might be. When we need strength or encouragement, it's there for us in big doses.

All we have to do is add a little water.

THE MOST IMPORTANT THING IS THE MESSAGE, NOT THE MESSENGER

The two most important people in my early recovery were my original sponsor and his wife. If I had a Sobriety Hall of Fame, they would be chartering members.

They were the ones who came on a twelfth-step call when I crashed and burned and wound up in the hospital. They were the ones who arranged for me to go to rehab, and the ones who were there for me when I got back out into the real world again.

They taught me the program, step by step. They opened up their house to me, morning, noon, and night. They worked and worked and worked with me. They absolutely insisted on being happy, joyous, and free, and they made early sobriety fun. They loved me, and for maybe the first time in my life, they made me feel loved. They listened to me whine, they talked me down off the cliff a few times, they encouraged me to keep going, and they truly gave me hope. They told me it was okay. They told me I was okay.

Most of all, they convinced me that the program worked, although they said it a little differently. "It works if you work it," she always said.

I believed every word they said, and it motivated me to work the program to the absolute best of my ability.

And then, about two years into my sobriety, they fell off the pedestal. With a thud.

Their marriage began falling apart, and I found out some things that made me feel angry, confused, heartbroken, even a bit betrayed. It turned out they weren't always walking like they talked. You could say that they were just plain hypocrites in a lot of ways. All these principles and ideals that they instilled in me, they weren't actually living themselves. This big, wonderful, happy family that their other sponsees and I felt a part of was actually dysfunctional as hell.

I did the only thing I knew to do at that point. I got indignant. I got self-righteous. I disowned them and got myself a new sponsor, a no-nonsense guy that I knew did everything by the book. I completely broke away from them and swore that I would never be so hypocritical.

Eventually, she started drinking again and wound up dying of cirrhosis of the liver; he moved far away never to be heard of again, and I never got over it for a long, long time.

Folks in the program would tell you that the moral of this story is to never put anyone on a pedestal. We all have clay feet, as *The Big Book* says. We all have our issues, and we are all human, and when we rely on humans, it is perhaps inevitable that they will let us down.

But I can look back at the situation today with a completely different set of glasses.

You see, there have been times in my sobriety since then that I have been every bit as hypocritical as they were in various ways. I have not always walked like I talked. I have practiced these principles in 85 percent of my affairs but not in all my affairs. I have done stupid things, regrettable things, hardly in the mode of doing God's will or doing the next right thing. I have fooled myself into justifying a lot of things, especially in a stretch where I wasn't going to many meetings at all.

Not that anyone has ever put me on a pedestal, but if they did, I most certainly would have fallen off it too. With a thud.

Makes me a lot less critical of others when my own human frailties surface. Makes me a lot more forgiving when I realize I'm surely not anywhere near perfect myself. Makes me grateful for second chances, for a program that stresses progress, not perfection.

I am mindful of something else too.

The message is the most important thing. Thank God they carried the message and taught me the fundamentals and gave me the wonderful foundation they gave me, even if they weren't always walking the walk. Thank God they smothered me with love at a time when I needed it desperately, even if they weren't practicing these principles in all their affairs. Thank God they came into my life when they did.

I can say with no reservation that my first year of sobriety was the best year of my life—as I felt a new freedom and a new happiness—and for all their warts they were the ones most responsible.

Today I shoot for higher ideals than ever. Today I am closer to practicing these principles in all my affairs more than perhaps ever, because I have hopefully learned from my mistakes. I'm not the same person I was before I got sober, for sure, and I'm not even the person I was ten years ago when I was away from the program and putting my job and several other things ahead of my sobriety. It feels good to be able to say that.

But even if I stumble, it's important that I continue to carry the message. It's important to give others hope that yes, the program does work, if you work it. Sure, it's best when you talk the talk and walk the walk at the same time, but there's still something to be said for passing it on under whatever the circumstances.

They proved that, and their impact remains. I am no longer indignant. I am forever grateful.

THERE ARE SUCH UNFORTUNATES, THEY SEEM TO HAVE BEEN BORN THAT WAY

There was a guy that came to one of my favorite meetings a few years back who was in and out and in and out and in and out, never building up any substantial sobriety.

He was a strange bird. He would go off topic during meetings and share all sorts of bizarre stories, many that were difficult for me to believe. He had no people skills to speak of, with a way of saying the wrong thing to the wrong person at the wrong time. It was clear that he was not grasping even the most basic tenets of the program. The best thing I could say about him was that he kept coming back.

Then after another in a long string of failures, he asked me to be his sponsor.

Of course I said yes, even though I can't say that I was all too excited about it. I was encouraged that he could at least see that some kind of change was necessary and that he could at least embrace the concept of sponsorship. My original sponsor's wife used to have a saying, "If you keep doing what you're doing, you'll keep getting what you're getting," and what he had been doing clearly wasn't working.

I laid out five must-dos. Don't drink. Go to meetings. Read *The Big Book*. Pray. Call your sponsor or another alcoholic.

Well, he got at least two of them right—go to meetings and call your sponsor.

He called, and he called, and he called. He blew up my phone like no sponsee ever had, several times a day. Usually, it wasn't about any particular problem he was having; he was just calling to talk. I would try to steer the conversation to spiritual matters or the steps occasionally, but that wasn't always the case, and it certainly wasn't always successful by any means.

I have to say, it was the most frustrating experience I have ever had with a sponsee. I don't think I ever had that full conviction that he could get sober and stay sober, and that might have been part of the problem too. We never got past the first three steps, and honestly, I'm not sure that he ever fully took any of the steps.

Eventually, the inevitable happened. He drank again, even against a doctor's warning that he would die of cirrhosis of the liver if he did. He would still come to meetings occasionally, and in the weeks to follow, we watched the horrors of the final stages of alcoholism unfold. His skin turned yellow, literally, before our very eyes. Then one day came word that he had died.

Only then did it occur to me, this was a person who had been constitutionally incapable of being honest with himself, someone who could not—not would not—completely give himself to this simple program.

The Big Book says there are such unfortunates, that they are not at fault, that they seem to have been born that way. But I had never truly believed it. I had always believed that anyone who could look in the mirror could get honest with themselves, especially if they made the commitment to go to any lengths. I thought *The Big Book* was talking about mentally retarded people, or those with extreme cases of schizophrenia or other mental illness.

It wasn't until his final dying days that I learned to be compassionate, because only then was I able to see him for who he really was—a screwed-up, tortured soul who had lived a pathetic life, who had been called a loser all his life by his family, who didn't know how to make friends, who wanted desperately to fit in, who was just wanting someone to tell him he was okay.

Isn't there a little bit (or a lot) of that in all of us?

It punctuated something we say in the program. We're not bad people trying to get good; we're sick people trying to get well. It's just that he never got well.

I can't say that I'm as compassionate to everyone as I need to be. I still get angered by some people in the program, especially when I watch them hurt others. But I do, at least, have moments of clarity and compassion, and I do firmly believe that we're all in this together. And I better see the value of the fellowship, if for no other reason than to let everyone feel part of.

It reminds me, too, that "there but for the grace of God go I." Truth is, once I hit bottom, God made it very easy for me to get sober. I embraced the program and all sorts of good things started happening almost immediately. I could see the program working in my life early on, and that motivated me to work even harder, and the better I worked the program, the more positive results I got.

For that, I am so grateful.

THAT GUY NAMED GOD SURE
HAS A SENSE OF HUMOR

One thing we can say with certainty about God as we understand Him is this—He definitely has a sense of humor.

There are countless examples, obviously, but none better for me than the night I did my first fifth step and then the sixth and seventh steps in the hour following.

I had finally crashed and burned in the previous month, wound up in the hospital initially, and then in rehab for the most important thirty days of my life.

Throughout my adult years, I had been one of those folks who had conveniently put God on the side burner and figured I would deal with all that stuff later in life. I had always had an inferiority complex when it came to religion; I'd never had an epiphany or seen a burning bush, so I figured something was wrong, something was missing. It wasn't a matter of denying God's existence; it was just a matter of blotting the whole subject out and not dealing with it.

The steps forced me to deal with it. And fortunately, they gave me the perfect way to deal with it.

The second step allowed me to ease into the concept of spirituality. I wasn't ready to turn my will and life over to the care of God as we understood him right off the bat, but I didn't have to. That's the third step. That comes later. What I could do immediately was acknowledge that I wasn't the center of the universe, that there was indeed a power greater than myself. And *The Big Book* said, all it took was a small crack in the door to get started. Did I believe there was a higher power, or was I willing to try to believe? Of course, the answer was yes.

Truth is that God started working in my life very quickly once I entered rehab. *The Big Book* spoke to me. I related so much to ever paragraph, every sentence. The lectures made sense, and the meetings we attended were so powerful. God was, in fact, restoring me to sanity before my very eyes. So when it came time to do the third step, I was ready. It hit me—my higher power is God, not some doorknob or tree or the ever-famous Group of Drunks. And if I acknowledged that God existed, I would be a fool not to turn my will and life over to Him. I had already seen just how far the alternative had gotten me.

A huge key to the third step for me was the clause, "God as we understood Him." I realized that I didn't understand Him very well, but that was okay. How could I, after drinking alcoholically the previous fifteen years and keeping Him at arm's distance throughout? So I kind of threw out all the things I had religious hang-ups over—Noah's Ark, the Book of Revelation, certain things about Jesus, etc.—and just tried to start a one-on-one relationship with God as my foundation. I didn't understand God much at all, but I had some basics, and I could build on it from there.

So where does God's sense of humor come in?

Precisely here. By the time my final night in rehab rolled around, I had indeed taken the third step with all its ramifications. I was proceeding on with the steps with the notion that it was all right that I hadn't seen the burning bush, that God would reveal what needed to be revealed in due time.

So in the hour after doing my fifth step, I did as *The Big Book* said and went outside to be alone all to myself, praying and meditating and going over everything that had happened in the previous thirty days to make sure my foundation was solid.

I was sitting on a bench outside the dorm. It was a pleasant evening in early May, some clouds but some stars. I was confident that I had worked each of the steps to the best of my ability, that there were no half-measures along the way. I was ready to get out of rehab, ready to go back to the real world and start my new life. I was totally at peace, with the feeling of serenity (and relief) that comes to anybody who has just taken a thorough fifth step.

And lo and behold, suddenly there was a flash of heat lightning.

And a few seconds later, another flash of heat lightning.

And suddenly, I was catching on and zeroing in on the fact that the heat lightning behind the clouds made the clouds look like, yes, a burning bush.

It continued for several minutes, one flash after another, and it got to the point that I had to start laughing. It was as if God was saying, "Well, you wanted a burning bush, here it is."

Truth is, I got my burning bush *after* I had come to peace with the fact that I didn't need to see a burning bush in order to develop a relationship with God. When I made the decision to start from scratch and not make any demands on Him, He had a little surprise for me.

Time and time again in my sobriety, I have had examples of God being twenty thousand steps ahead of me, and this was certainly one of them. A very important one of them. No doubt He got a chuckle out of it like I did. When times are tough, or I think God is not around or not working in my life, I have to remember that night.

I have seen heat lightning in the clouds. Sounds like a burning bush to me.

NO MATTER WHAT IS SAID AT A MEETING, SOMEONE NEEDS TO HEAR IT

One of the most influential people in my recovery over the years has been a friend named Jeff.

He had tons of sobriety when I met him and just a wonderful amount of wisdom on all sorts of topics, including *The Big Book* and especially life itself.

He became well-known throughout the recovery community for ending each of his shares with, "If nobody has told you they love you today, I do," and that was precisely the way he was.

I have to say, without question, he was the embodiment of everything that is good about the program. He loved helping people. He lived a happy, joyous, and free lifestyle, with true serenity 99 percent of the time. He had been through much, including the death of one of his children, and yet he had used all the tragic events of his life to try to comfort others and carry the message.

So there was this night when he started to share during a meeting, and he talked and talked and talked and talked. And he just kept going, and he started repeating himself, and he went on and on and on, and all this great sobriety he always shared was suddenly turning into blah, blah, blah, blah, blah in my ears.

I remember sitting there saying to myself, "All right, Jeff, we've got it, you've said it over and over, how about wrapping it up and letting someone else share?"

As good a friend as he was, as much respect as I had for him, I was starting to tune him out.

So it finally happened. After what had to be at least twenty minutes, he ended with, "If nobody has told you they love you today, I do," and we went on with the meeting.

And that should have been the end of it.

But afterward, we were talking, and suddenly, he mentioned that he was going into the hospital the following morning for heart bypass surgery. That's the reason, he said, why he had so much to talk about and get out of his system. He needed to make sure he was right with God, he needed to reinforce to himself that it was all going to work out the way it was supposed to work out.

I felt terrible for tuning him out. It quickly occurred to me, if I was going to have heart bypass surgery the next morning, I would be at a meeting, and I would talk and talk and talk and talk too. I would need all the spiritual strength and faith that I could muster. And I most certainly would need the support of my best friends.

Since that night, I have been less inclined to tune people out when they share or to be so judgmental of their shares. I know now that there is more than meets the eye when it comes to people and their problems. My sponsor has a saying, "No matter what is said at a meeting, someone needs to hear it," and that is so, so true. Sometimes, that might even be the person who is doing the talking.

So the lesson is open-mindedness, which is so vital in 12-step recovery. If we're open to the fact that there might be more than meets the eye, we can position ourselves to be more understanding, or more helpful, or more supportive, or whatever the case may be. And if we're open-minded when it comes to meetings, then we should be able to carry over that open-mindedness to any number of issues or walks of life.

Jeff died a few years back, and he has been sorely missed by everyone that knew him. But he definitely left a legacy, left his imprint on all the meetings in the area. Whenever somebody rambles on at a meeting, I immediately think of him. If nobody has told you they love you today, he does.

THE EMOTIONS AND EPIPHANIES OF ENDURING A ROOT CANAL

A root canal.

I had never experienced one, but I had heard all the horror stories, and I had always cringed at the notion of what one might feel like if the day ever came when it was necessary. I'm not good with pain. Having my wisdom teeth extracted and having a couple of crowns was as far as I ever wanted to go.

But here I sat in a strange dentist's chair, and suddenly, I was facing reality that the dreaded day had finally come. I had awakened that morning with terrible pain in one of my front lower teeth, needed relief fast because I was scheduled to travel internationally the very next day. My regular dentist was totally booked for the day, so I had to find a dentist that could work a walk-in into his schedule.

The guy took X-rays, then was blunt. No, it wasn't simply a matter of gum disease that could be easily remedied. No, it wasn't a matter of putting in a filling. The tooth was totally infected, totally shot, and there were only three options. A root canal. An extraction. Or I could do nothing and let the situation get worse and worse and worse.

In other words, there was really only one option.

It would be an understatement to say that my heart sank. I was instantly filled with fear, conjuring up all sorts of images of how much pain was going to be involved. I tried to negotiate, both in my mind and with the dentist, hoping against hope that there was some solution other than a root canal. I sat there momentarily in shock that my day could be impacted so negatively by such an unexpected turn of events.

When the dentist quoted me a price of $1,172 for the procedure, since I had to pay cash, the emotions swirled even more. I was mad at myself for not taking better care of my teeth, since this obviously could have been prevented, and just overwhelmed that such bad news on so many levels could come completely out of the blue.

What happened in the next hour or so proved to be an amazingly poignant experience.

As the procedure began, I started to realize that I was going to have to accept what was happening whether I liked it or not. I started to realize that I was now powerless over the situation and that I was going to have to make it through the next hour regardless of how much pain I was in for, no matter how much I didn't want to be sitting there in that dentist's chair.

I had to muster up the courage to make it through the procedure, period. I had to deal with the adversity of it all, and I had to be an adult about it. Crosby, Stills, and Nash sing a song that goes, "Rejoice, rejoice, we have no choice but to carry on," and I was going to have to live those lyrics, not just sing them.

The good news is that being in a 12-step program and trying to live a life of sobriety had prepared me for the situation. Acceptance is one of the many tools in the recovery toolbox that we can summon up for strength in times like this. Acceptance allows us to tap into a reservoir that gives us both courage and comfort. It's one of our ultimate coping mechanisms. I said the Serenity Prayer several times in that dentist's chair, and more than that, I came to understand that the momentary pain I was going through would ultimately be beneficial for me in the long run.

I don't want to say I had a major epiphany, but I also realized that what I was going through was small potatoes compared to those who are undergoing chemotherapy or dialysis or are dealing with life-and-death medical issues. Those are the truly courageous people, the ones who didn't do anything to bring about their diseases and maladies but hang in there because they have no other choice.

In the big picture, this whole experience will serve me well, even if it was an expensive lesson. There can be adversity in our lives that we don't deserve and don't bring on, but then there are unforced errors and that was definitely the case here. I should have taken better care of my teeth, and I would have never been in this predicament. I need to change the things I can, as the Serenity Prayer says.

And surely, I will run into bigger challenges and more curve balls later in life as I grow older. If we're lucky enough to reach old age, it's inevitable that our bodies will break down, and we'll have to deal with far worse than root canals. I don't know if I'll one day get cancer or have a heart attack or whatever, but I know there will come a time when I'm going to have to accept something major that I can't change, and I'm going to have to call on God for strength and courage. I'm going to have to carry on.

This is a huge reminder, too, that unexpected events can happen in the blink of an eye, and so we need to appreciate all our blessings and never take anything for granted.

By the way, the root canal wasn't painless, but it wasn't nearly as painful as I had feared. The guy did a great job numbing it up, and once I started taking medication to clear up the infection, my whole body started feeling better. Somebody must have been looking out for me.

FEAR OF PEOPLE AND OF ECONOMIC INSECURITY WILL LEAVE US

When I was early in sobriety, and first read the ninth-step promises, I spotted a few that I thought would probably come true.

But there were others that I wondered about, and even if I could see them eventually coming true, I thought they would be a long, long way off.

One in particular was, "Fear of people and of economic insecurity will leave us."

I was in so much debt when I got sober that I couldn't comprehend any way I would get back on my feet very quickly. I had been living paycheck to paycheck in my drinking days, bouncing checks on Wednesday to get the money to buy liquor until payday on Friday. All my credit cards had been shut off. I never missed any meals, but it was a meager existence.

Sure, just by getting sober, I was saving the substantial sum that went to buying my booze each week, but it seemed like throwing a deck chair off the Titanic.

So how did the fear of economic insecurity leave me?

It's a wonderful story, and it is a testament to working the program the right way.

When I got to the ninth step, "Made direct amends to such people wherever possible, except when to do so would injure them or others," *The Big Book* was very emphatic about addressing finances and cleaning up past debts. There was to be no running from it, no exceptions. This "suggestion" was really a command.

One of the things hanging over my head at the time was the fact that I hadn't filed my taxes for the previous four or five years. Part of that was because of sheer laziness. But part was based on the fear that I would owe the government and wouldn't have the money to pay.

I had always taken a true alcoholic's approach: ignore it and pretend that maybe it'll go away.

But now, if I was to work the steps, if I was to practice these principles in all my affairs, if I was going to show that I truly was willing to go to any lengths, it was time to address the situation regardless of what happened.

I went to a counseling agency that contacted my credit card companies and worked on repayment options without any more late fees or penalties.

Then it was time to deal with the back taxes

I made the decision that the only thing to do was to file them and let the cards fall as they may. If I owed thousands, I would just have to own up to it and try to pay the government off the same way I would the credit cards.

The counseling agency filled out all the forms for me, we sent them in…and then it happened.

It turned out that my employers had taken out way more than they should have, and even with all the fees and penalties, I was owed a very big refund. When the refund came, I was able to pay off all the credit cards, and there was plenty left. Suddenly, I had gone from deep in debt to being back on my feet again.

And voila, the fear of economic uncertainty had left me.

Not that I built up a huge fortune in the ensuing months, or even years for that matter. It still took time to get all my finances truly in order and get to where I could start saving.

But I had hope. I was no longer weighed down by major debt. And I had seen the promise come true, right before my very eyes, a promise that seemed so unlikely when I got into the program.

There are lessons, of course. One is that these folks who wrote *The Big Book* really do know what they're talking about. If they say something, you can take it to the bank (hah!). Another is that if you confront your problems head-on, the outcome might be a little better than you expect. But it takes action.

Truth is the fear of economic insecurity returns from time to time. When the stock market collapsed a few years back, I definitely was freaked out like the rest of the country. When I got laid off from my newspaper job of twenty-one years, I wondered what the future would hold, and there was some fear tugging at my faith. I'm not sure how long my retirement fund will last once I quit working.

But at the same time, I have tangible examples in my life of the promises coming true that I can always fall back on. I have stories like the back taxes that remind me that if I do what's in front of me, chances are it will all work out.

Grateful I am for that.

SINGING "YELLOW SUBMARINE" WITH RINGO? ANYTHING'S POSSIBLE

Last year, I did one of the neatest things I've ever done in my lifetime.

I sang "Hey Jude" with Paul McCartney.

Of course, there were fifty thousand others doing the same thing on a wonderful night at Met Life Stadium in East Rutherford, New Jersey., but that's beside the point. It was magical, and it was the fulfillment of a dream that would have seemed impossible back when I was growing up as a huge Beatles fan in the sixties.

It came on the heels of visiting the Beatles Museum in Liverpool earlier last summer and taking a ride on the Magical Mystery Tour with stops at Strawberry Fields and the Cavern Club and other various Beatles landmarks. Liverpool is so neat, and there is just such a positive vibe in the air everywhere you go.

Next month comes a trip to Las Vegas to sing "Yellow Submarine" with Ringo Starr and his All-Starr Band, and I'm sure it's going to be great as well.

This is all a tribute to the fact that, yes, just about anything is possible in life.

If you would have told me when I was a kid that one day I would be making annual trips to London and spending afternoons at Abbey Road, or that I would ride through the middle of the roundabout on Penny Lane, or that I would be singing with Paul and Ringo, I would never have believed it.

I have to be totally honest. The Beatles had a much bigger influence on me than they ever should have. And they probably have a bigger influence on me today than back when I was growing up.

They have provided the soundtrack to my life ever since I watched them on the Ed Sullivan Show for the first time.

I laugh now at the folks who labeled them as demons when John said they were bigger than Jesus, which he later acknowledged was a stupid thing to say, because there is so much spirituality in so many of their songs. When I find myself in times of trouble, Mother Mary comes to me, speaking words of wisdom, let it be. That's Paul. John is, no place you can be that isn't where you're meant to be, all you need is love.

The part I focus on is that I am doing things that I could never have imagined possible, and it's all due to sobriety.

Remember, there was a time during my drinking years when I was living in a rathole apartment, was living paycheck to paycheck, bouncing checks on Wednesday to get enough liquor to last me until payday on Friday, had all my credit cards cut off, and was simply a pathetic person. Back then, the closest I was going to get to the Beatles was my record player. And I was a pretty hopeless person, so there was no expectation of anything ever getting better.

Yet now, I have not only been to Liverpool, but I have the ability to get on a plane and go again anytime I get the urge. I don't know for sure, but I think I'm coming up on maybe twenty-five trips to Europe at this point all told.

I am so grateful.

ABOUT THE AUTHOR

John Delong is a retired sportswriter living in Charlotte, North Carolina.

He spent twenty-one years working for the *Winston-Salem Journal*, covering the NBA's Charlotte Hornets for twelve years and the NFL's Carolina Panthers for six and, at other times, covering college basketball, college football, and professional golf and tennis.

He has also worked for the ATP's Winston-Salem Open tennis tournament and was a sports travel agent and tour guide, taking groups to such sporting events as Wimbledon, the Masters, the Ryder Cup, and the US Open golf and tennis tournaments.

He has also done freelance work for *The Sporting News*, the Associated Press, and several newspapers around the country.

Most importantly, he has stayed sober for almost four decades and is active in Charlotte's 12-step recovery community. He has a sponsor, and he is a sponsor, and he is deeply grateful to have God's grace throughout the years.

9 798893 151480